Redefining Sustainable Development

Redefining Sustainable Development

Neil Middleton and Phil O'Keefe

First published 2001 by Pluto Press
345 Archway Road, London N6 5AA
and 22883 Quicksilver Drive, Sterling, VA 20166-2012, USA

www.plutobooks.com

British Library of Cataloguing in Publication Data
A catalogue record for this book is available from the British Library

Library of Congress Cataloging-in-Publication Data

Middleton, Neil.
  Redefining sustainable development / Neil Middleton and Phil O'Keefe
    p. cm.
  ISBN 0-7453-1610-7 (hardback)
  1. Sustainable development. 2. Non-governmental organisations. 3.
Social classes. I. O'Keefe, Philip. II. Title.
  HC79.E5 M463 2001
  338.9'27—dc21
          00-009443

  ISBN 978 0 7453 1605 5 paperback

Designed and produced for Pluto Press by
Chase Publishing Services, Fortescue, Sidmouth EX10 9QG
Typeset from disk by Gawcott Typesetting Services

Printed and bound by CPI Group (UK) Ltd, Croydon, CR0 4YY

Contents

List of Tables and Figures

Tables

Figures

ETC

This book is an ETC project. Founded in The Netherlands in 1974 and now established in India, Sri Lanka, Kenya, Britain and Ireland, ETC exists to encourage and support local initiatives towards sustainable development. It is organised under the umbrella of ETC International which is located in The Netherlands. It recognises that local knowledge and experience are the building blocks for any developmental activity and that those communities for whom aid projects of any kind are constructed must have substantial influence on their design. Employing people from many and varied backgrounds, ETC can offer expertise in sustainable agriculture, agroforestry, energy, water supplies, humanitarian assistance, institutional development and training and extension courses. For further information write to ETC UK, 117 Norfolk Street, North Shields, Tyne and Wear NE30 1NQ.

Acknowledgements

We are grateful, as always, for the support of and comments from Di Jelley and from our colleagues in ETC UK, Donna Porter and John Kirkby. Particular thanks are also due to Geraldine Mitchell, whose editorial skills have saved us from several errors. Trojan work by John Plunkett and Martin McGuire of Connect Ireland Communications Ltd (www.connect.ie) rescued the text of this book from oblivion following a particularly violent viral attack on our computers, we are grateful to them for saving us a year's work. Our thanks, too, to Gemma Marren whose careful copy-editing frequently rescued us from our own carelessness. Any errors in the text are entirely our own.

Abbreviations and Acronyms

ALNAP	Active Learning Network on Accountability and Performance in Humanitarian Aid
BNA	Basic Needs Approach
CAFOD	Catholic Fund for Overseas Development
CAP	Common Agricultural Policy
CARE	Cooperative Agency for Relief Everywhere
CBA	cost-benefit analysis
CIA	Central Intelligence Agency
DIGNAS	*Mujeres por la Dignidad y la Vida* (Women for Dignity and Life)
ERM	Exchange Rate Mechanism
ERT	European Round Table of Industrialists
EU	European Union
FDI	foreign direct investment
FMLN	Farabundo Martí Front for National Liberation
GATS	General Agreement on Trade in Services
GATT	General Agreement on Tariffs and Trade
GEMS	Global Environmental Monitoring System
GM	genetically modified
GDP	gross domestic product
GNP	gross national product
HDI	human development index (originated by the UNDP)
HPI	human poverty index (originated by the UNDP)
ICIDI	Independent Commission on Development Issues
IFI	international financial institution
ILEIA	Institute for Low External Input Agriculture

IMF	International Monetary Fund
INGO	international non-governmental organisation
IUCN	International Union for the Conservation of Nature and Natural Resources
LEEC	London Environmental Economics Centre
LEISA	low external input and sustainable agriculture
MAI	Multilateral Agreement on Investment
MSF	*Médecins sans Frontières*
MVs	modern varieties
NAFTA	North American Free Trade Association
NGO	non-governmental organisation
NGDO	non-governmental development organisations
NIC	Newly Industrialised Country
NTAE	non-traditional agricultural export
ODI	Overseas Development Institute
OECD	Organisation for Economic Cooperation and Development
OED	*Oxford English Dictionary*
OPEC	Organisation of Petroleum Exporting Countries
PADF	Pan-American Development Foundation
PPP$	parity purchasing power (measured in US dollars)
SANGOCO	South African National NGO Coalition
SILIC	severely indebted low income country (originated by the World Bank)
SLORC	State Law and Order Restoration Council
SPDC	State Peace and Development Council
TNC	transnational corporation
UNCED	United Nations Conference on Environment and Development
UNDP	United Nations Development Programme
UNEP	United Nations Environment Programme
UNFCCC	*United Nations Framework Convention on Climate Change*
UNICEF	United Nations Children's Fund
URL	Uniform Resource Locator
USAID	United States' Agency for International Development
WCED	World Commission on Environment and Development ('Brundtland Commission')
WRI	World Resources Institute
WTO	World Trade Organisation

1

Introduction: The Rich Wage War, The Poor Die

(apologies to Sartre[1])

The acceptance of globalisation, of universal neo-liberalism, particularly by much of the left, has allowed its consolidation to go
uncontested. In promoting their world view, Clinton–Blair–Giddens
have silenced the reactionary right, but only at the cost of striking
dumb the struggle for social justice. Democratic rights are not a
substitute for social justice and social justice itself cannot be delivered without tackling property relations – for that purpose we have
to create a deeply embedded network of collective institutions for
the twenty-first century.

An essential part of that creative process must be to address the
issues of sustainability, particularly in the matter of rights to global
commons. Ultimately, this will mean organising against, challenging
and transcending the globalising dialogue. We accept Goldman's
point that strong states are not simply being replaced by markets,
tradition by modernity and the local by the global.[2] Quoting
Hadaway,[3] he argues that 'local' does not mean provincial, limited or
unscientific understanding, but understanding which is located,
situated and partial; 'global' does not mean universal, general and
apolitical understanding, but understanding which is distributed,
layered and equally partial. Both understandings demand realism
not epistemological relativism. This is why we explore, no matter
how briefly, cultural canons as well as case material in order to criticise transnational corporations (TNCs) and international financial
institutions (IFIs). That approach also makes us question that *dea ex*

machina, the international NGOs (INGOs) who see themselves as the solutions, as civil society and as the fountain of good governance.

Both the authors of this book were engaged in and around the debate of the '10 Years after Stockholm', held in Nairobi in 1982, and one of them was present at it. It was the occasion when the global powers, under a Reagan–Thatcher hegemony, reviewed environmental progress, or rather the lack of it.[4] The centre of attention was the United Nations Environment Programme (UNEP), locally translated as the United Nations Egyptian Programme (since its director, at the time, was M.W. Kassas, an Egyptian national) or sometimes, more appropriately given its lack of impact, the United Nations Entertainment Programme. UNEP had offered, as its two striking successes, its Global Environmental Monitoring System (GEMS) and its Regional Seas Programme. Since neither of them had much to do with people and their problems, we feel that they hardly add up to a success. But during this environmental menagerie, one of us was invited to two famous meals in which the future of global environmental policy was determined.

The first, a dinner party given by a member of the Swedish Embassy, was a rather splendid affair and the splendour was in the conversation. It was about creating, and maintaining in being, a social-democratic global initiative linking environment and development, which should be financed separately from both the UN system and the Reagan–Thatcher axis and beyond the control of either. Representatives of the Nordic countries present at that dinner applauded the idea as it emerged and declared themselves to be strongly in favour of it. That conversation subsequently led to the creation of the Brundtland Commission, the World Commission on Environment and Development (WCED). The second was a private lunch in which a leading American scholar informed us that the US had already decided to respond to global environmental issues, also quite separately from the United Nations. A leading research institute, funded by the MacArthur Foundation, was to be established; it is now known as the World Resources Institute (WRI). The environment had suddenly become politics.

Sustainability was at the centre of the Brundtland Commission's work. The concept was deliberately ill-defined to prevent unnecessary and destructive objections and much of this book is concerned with the problems produced by that diplomatic vagueness. Three broad areas of concern were covered by the Commission – ecological, economic and social – and each of them brought its own agenda. Ecologists were driven by the work of the International Union for the Conservation of Nature and Natural Resources (IUCN) which, guided by the second law of thermodynamics, addressed the tendency of systems to be entropic. They sought to maintain ecological sustainability by maintaining the complexity and variability of systems, by emphasising the non-reducibility of organisms and by paying attention to uncertainty, spontaneity and collectivity in nature. Economists looked at the environment as so much capital stock and pushed a form of analysis, macro and micro, that proposed the polluter (user) pays principle. Social concern amounted to little more than nice words designed to lower expectations, but little guidance to building stable, resilient and equitable communities was offered.

After the Brundtland Report and its follow-up, the United Nations Conference on Environment and Development (UNCED), these areas of concern have consolidated. Ecological concern focuses primarily on rural issues and the global commons without paying very much attention to urban settlements where most people live. The denial of urbanisation, a product of the romantic tradition which we discuss at greater length in Chapter 3, is found well beyond what is commonly understood to be 'literary' work. Glacken's *Traces on the Rhodian Shore*[5] and, more paradoxically, Hoskins' *The Making of the English Landscape*,[6] both came abruptly to an end when they arrived at the Industrial Revolution and its attendant urbanisation. It took E.P. Thompson, mimicking Hoskins' title, to carry the tale forward in *The Making of the English Working Class*, in which he abandoned rural idylls for urban reality.[7] Nature, for Thompson's predecessors, was everything not industrialised or urbanised, a mistaken view still pursued by much of today's environmental movement.

Similarly, economic concern was reduced to a very particular economic argument – external costs, resource exhaustion, discounted cash-flows, common property, valuation, regulation and cost-benefit analysis all led to an understanding of the environment as a market problem, not to an analysis of the market as an environmental problem.[8]

Social issues, which should have focused on community, failed to emerge, not least because Brundtland tried to square the circle of ecological and economic concerns by arguing for growth with equity – the infamous canard of 'trickle down'. We confront the issue of social justice and its meanings and address those organisations, particularly international non-governmental organisations (INGOs), which frequently claim to provide solutions. Table 1 summarises the argument and the logic of this book; it is, after all, our way of seeing our world and its future.

Table 1.1 Themes of sustainability

Theme	Ecology	Economics	Social Development
Policy aims	Biodiversity, avoidance of system collapse	Market prices for environmental goods	Stability, equity
Problems of intervention	Nature is not pristine, but constructed	Markets do not reflect value	Communities are destroyed, and built, by market forces

It is first necessary for us to set out the bones of the problems that we are addressing. Some adjectives, or adjectival phrases, have become so embedded in their nouns as to render them almost nugatory; thus all communists are 'card-carrying', all Catholics 'devout' and all development 'sustainable'. No longer adjectival in popular speech, these words have become parts of their nouns. Communists and Catholics may look after themselves, in this book we are concerned with the assumptions made when the words 'sustainable development' are uttered in the context of relations between the industrialised and *soi-disant* 'developing' worlds. For some theorists they are a pleonasm since development which is not sustainable is not development, for those who see most, if not all, development as exploitative it is an oxymoron; there can be none for whom the expression is not an ideological battlefield. Since the world hovers perennially on the edge of massive financial recession and, not infrequently, begins to tip over it, we are forced to examine at least some of the meanings attached to development and, in particular, to sustainability. It is, after all, the poor who suffer the most from financial disaster, just as they suffer from every other kind.

In recent years, a morally mildly repugnant question has arisen – what is the collective noun for poor countries? 'Third World' is preserved as a political label by many radicals within it although they are busy redefining the phrase.[9] It is, for that reason, viewed with nervousness or distaste by those who would prefer to tame theory by depoliticising it. 'Poor countries', 'severely indebted low income countries (SILICs)', 'high human poverty index (HPI) countries' or 'low human development index (HDI) countries' are among the many that have been offered and become controversial because they have been found patronising. With what we may legitimately regard as a crude sense of satire, there are those, still, who talk and write of 'developing countries'.[10] Recent summary figures demonstrate, yet again, the depressing contradiction contained in this misnomer (see table 1.2). These figures are little more than a guide; they conceal, for example, the substantial disparities between rich and poor in all the regions they cover, including the 'industrial countries'. Nonetheless they demonstrate the ways in which, despite marginal absolute improvements, the relative difference between rich and poor has not lessened and, in some cases, has actually increased. We, like many others, commented on this long ago and see no reason now to change the judgement we made in 1993:

> For the last few years it has made no sense to talk of 'developing' countries – huge parts of the world are now spinning down into national collapse and destruction involving misery, starvation and death for immense numbers of ordinary people ... we ... see not merely the ludicrous disparities, the hopeless distances to be made up, but also the chronicle of a situation rapidly worsening.[11]

The centripetal nature of capital has produced a politics and an economics of exclusion. Phenomena like 'fortress Europe', the US failure to honour even its financial obligations to the UN and the growing divisions between rich and poor within the industrialised world, as well as between rich and poor countries, are all examples. We shall return, indirectly, to the arguments suggesting that this exclusivity is structural, that is to say, built into capital and its institutions. Here it is only necessary to point to a conceptual difficulty facing, in particular, INGOs. Whatever the economic policies or

Table 1.2   Comparative trends in private consumption of selected items, by region and population

Item	Year	Industrial states	Developing states[4]	Sub-Saharan Africa
Meat	1970	57	29	3
(million tons)	1995	95	103	6
Cereals	1970	91	382	27
(million tons)	1995	160	706	56
Total energy	1975	4338	1237	139
(mtoe)[1]	1994	5611	2893	241
Electricity (b.kh)[2]	1980	5026	1260	147
	1995	9300	3575	255
Petrol	1980	455	96	10
(million tons)	1995	582	188	15
Cars (millions)	1975	228	21	3
	1993	390	65	5
McDonald's	1991	11970	448	0
restaurants	1996	19198	1824	17
Comparative	1970	1044	2616	267
populations[3]	1995	1233	4394	551

Notes
1 Millions of tons of oil equivalent.
2 Billions of kilowatt hours.
3 Millions.
4 Discrepancies in population totals follow from insufficient data from certain states.
Source: *Human Development Report, 1998*, UNDP.

circumstances of the states at issue may be, the aim of development, the eradication of humanly disabling poverty, must, in some degree, involve substantial modernisation; that is, the admission of the world's poor to contemporary forms of production and to adequate levels of mass consumption. Figure 1.1 provides a startling image of how little the world's poor really consume. Modernisation is thus a challenge to the exclusivity of capital structures and is the source of the difficulty for the INGOs. Two major impediments stand in the way of recognising this. On the one hand there is a politically

Arab states	East Asia	S.E. Asia & Pacific	South Asia	Latin America & Carib.
2	8	3	3	10
5	53	8	8	23
20	142	41	112	33
49	236	82	212	57
67	407	102	180	306
287	1019	296	457	531
98	390	73	161	364
327	1284	278	576	772
12	11	8	6	48
27	38	19	13	72
2	0.5	2	2	12
10	7	7	6	27
0	123	113	0	212
69	489	409	3	837
128	882	289	724	280
251	1296	482	1198	464

powerful romantic nostalgia, which we shall examine in later chapters, which makes many otherwise progressive people shy away from what they understand to be involved in modernisation. It is a sort of utopianism, heavily influenced by writers like Thoreau, in which we feel that others should be helped to avoid the errors that we have made. On the other hand the extent to which we have been persuaded of the rightness of private entrepreneurism, a belief which ludicrously encompasses the forms of late capitalism, persuades us also that incorporation into the present order is the only way forward. The extent to which this is so may be observed from the rise of green movements. It is a phenomenon accompanying the growing strength of capitalism and, unengagingly, frequently reproduces its priorities. There are honourable exceptions, like the groups around the *CNS* agenda, but the overwhelming majority of them concentrate on interference with nature, but not on interference with people. Protests are mounted against genetically modified plants, but not, for example, against the human genome project. We shall examine the ideological separation of nature and people in Chapter 3.

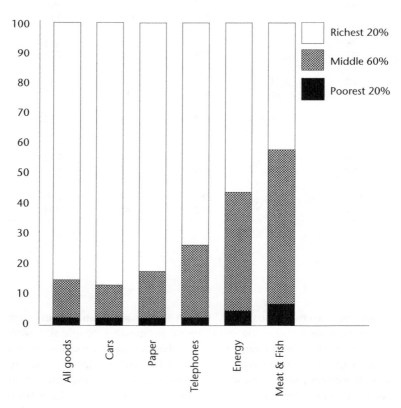

Figure 1.1   Patterns of unequal consumption

Source: Compiled from UNDP, 1998.

In his otherwise admirable book, *Striking a Balance*, Alan Fowler, writing about ways in which INGOs can be more effective, points out that it is wrong to suppose that 'economic growth is always good'. He goes on to say that development activity should be 'more holistic, people-centred ... unimpeded by the blinkering made necessary by IFI's limited economic mandates'. Social justice, the reduction of poverty leading 'to the growth and functioning of strong, autonomous organisations',[12] are the aims of development. These organisations, founded geographically and socially around the small projects for which they were created, will 'collaborate, associate and form other social structures within which they exert themselves' and thus have a profound effect on governance. In other words, they would be politicised and politicising. Fowler begins his analysis by looking first, and for this reason, at micro-projects in development, but in doing so overlooks the two principal difficulties in the way of widespread success.

The first difficulty is that of scale: even within a single, unitary, non-industrial state, organisations formed in this way would be tiny in number and would combine very slowly; worldwide the progress would be infinitesimal. In a way we feel that the model here may be that of early trade unionism, but if so, precisely because the unions emerged from rapidly industrialising societies, it is inappropriate. It is less than apt for another reason: in Britain it took trade unionism over two centuries from the repressive acts of 1719 and 1726[13] through the Combination Acts of 1799 and 1800,[14] to the smashing of the General Strike of 1926,[15] to achieve the relatively short-lived success of trade unionism from about 1946 until Margaret Thatcher's successful onslaught on it in the 1980s. There is no reason to suppose that the process would be much faster, or any less confrontational, in the societies that Fowler is considering. The second difficulty arises from the existing political and economic structures. These include repressive states commonly in pawn to what Fowler calls the IFIs; global agreements, frequently forced on weaker governments and backed by a body of international, even if dubious, law; and most importantly, *force majeure,* as in the war against Iraq designed, among other things, to protect the USA's hegemony in general and its control of oil and gas resources in particular. All these are in place precisely to circumvent the political threat to the stability of client regimes throughout the Third World which would be posed by the politicisation hoped for by Fowler. It is not our contention that these difficulties are insurmountable, merely that they must be recognised by INGOs for what they are – difficulties which are largely created by the very societies from which these international organisations, including INGOs, come.

It is possible, without too great an abuse of historical method, roughly to trace an ideological progression which has led to contemporary understandings of development. In the late sixteenth and early seventeenth centuries a number of philosophers, much influenced by Nicolaus Copernicus's cosmology and by Galileo Galilei's polemics in Italy's universities in support of new astronomies and physics, began to propose a new cosmogony. Among the most significant were Giordano Bruno (1548–1600), a monist who tried to identify an infinite universe with God and nature, and Tomasso Campanella (1568–1639) who, among other things, suggested that the study of nature in the light of reason would be the most fruitful means of improving the lot of humankind. For their pains, the Inquisition burnt the former and imprisoned the latter for very many years. A Spanish philosopher, Francisco Suárez (1548–1617), may also reasonably be seen as a founding father of much contemporary consciousness in his influential assertion that all reality is solely made up of individuals (he was, no doubt, Margaret Thatcher's bedside reading). These philosophers, late representatives of the Renaissance, prepared the ground for the emergence of that intellectual world in which an immutable natural and social order could be abandoned in favour of an individualism exemplified in the works of others like Descartes and, especially in the work of the German philosophers, Leibniz, Kant and Hegel.

Many people assume a simple historical progression from the rise of mercantilist capitalism in the late Renaissance, through the Industrial Revolution to modern capitalism, a progression marked by technological development which allows each new phase to come into being. But that history is far more complex than such a simple model would allow. The relationship between technology and social change is part of that complexity, and so, too, is the rise of the nation state. What the late nineteenth and the twentieth centuries produced was contemporary finance capitalism which bears little relationship, if any, to mercantilism. The ideological sea change that we have just sketched accompanied and, in a sense, validated the capitalist revolution in which it became possible to believe in John Stuart Mill's view that 'the very aim and object of action is to alter and improve Nature'.[16] It would not be entirely unreasonable to see this ambition as the means by which capital sold its tyranny to the people, but Marx, almost in response to something of the sort, magnificently made the crucial point that:

> Nature is man's *inorganic body*, that is to say nature in so far as it is not the human body. Man *lives* from nature, i.e. nature is his *body* and he must maintain a continuing dialogue with it if he is not to die. To say that man's physical and mental life is linked to nature simply means that nature is linked to itself, for man is a part of nature.

In the next paragraph he formulated a proposition that became fundamental to much of his life's work:

> Estranged labour not only (1) estranges nature from man and (2) estranges man from himself, from his own active function, from his vital activity; because of this it also estranges man from his *species*.[17]

We shall have occasion to return to this point, particularly in Chapter 3 where we first discuss David Harvey's major contribution to debate about this relationship in his book *Justice, Nature and the Geography of Difference*. The ground for this discussion is laid in Chapter 2 where we consider the ways in which nature has been socially produced and continues to be so by contemporary means and understandings and by, above all, capital.

Assumptions, not only about development, but about all its constituent parts, are made at countless levels and frequently differ widely. Development theory is dominated by a liberal (in the older sense) world view, even doughty defenders of those vast and commonly white-elephant enterprises visited on poverty-stricken countries make their cases in terms of their benefits to society at large. At the slightly less heroic end of development practice, local, communal advancement lies at the centre of most theory and activity based on a model of the kind illustrated in figure 1.2. Basing himself on Brown and Korten,[18] Wahab remarks that:

Development planners and policy makers have also realised that it is cost-effective to work with and through indigenous organizations on any development programme. The scope of development has also expanded to include ... a process by which members of a society develop themselves and their institutions in ways that enhance their ability to mobilize and manage resources to produce sustainable and justly distributed improvements in their quality of life.[19]

These sentiments are now virtually axiomatic, not only among development theorists and workers but even in the overseas development ministerial offices of most donor countries. Problems begin, however, when greater forces, for whom such sentiments are irrelevant, pursue other agendas. Such forces include the globalising marketeers with their client Ministers of Finance in each national treasury, their apparatus of world financial governance through the bourses, the international banks (including the World Bank and the International Monetary Fund – IMF), their supra-national trading agreements like the World Trade Organisation (WTO), the North American Free Trade Association (NAFTA), the European Union (EU) the Organisation for Cooperation and Development (OECD) and its long expected, but recently delayed, pup, the Multilateral Agreement on Investment (MAI)[20] and so on.

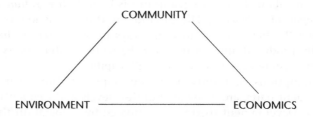

Figure 1.2   Mapping sustainability

Development for these powers means only further capital accumulation, that 'growth' on which their system depends. National functionaries in the industrialised world, the Chancellors of Exchequers, the Ministers of Finance, will always ensure that any other agenda is subservient to that end. Throughout the 'developing' world it is equally the case that there are few governments, if any, prepared to take another path – either they struggle to incorporate themselves into the relations of the global market in the desperate hope that their economies will strengthen sufficiently for them to compete, or, like the regimes of the late Sani Abacha in Nigeria or the State Law and Order Restoration Council (SLORC) of Burma,[21] they simply lapse into self-enriching and repressive oligarchies. Since the heyday of nineteenth-century imperialism, a few economic giants, other than the central powers, have loomed a little uncertainly into view; we may think of China, India and Brazil. Each of them has substantial resources, a huge population of cheap labour and rela-tively highly developed systems of governance. Brazil is quite possibly the most vulnerable of the three and may yet succumb to the malaise already afflicting Mexico, not the least because little has changed since Galeano first produced his magisterial analysis of Latin America in 1973.[22] Just how, if at all, these states will integrate into contemporary capitalism is still uncertain, nor, if they do, is it clear what effect they will have on the system. What is certain is that the TNCs, including occasional indigenous specimens, are scram-bling to stake their claims to what they see as burgeoning new markets and repositories of covetable resources.

Among social-democratic governments, globalising the 'free' market is usually accepted without question as a good and necessary process; its meaning is rarely addressed (we shall look more closely at it in Chapter 4) and its obvious and catastrophic weaknesses are ignored with ostrich-like insouciance by governments and financial traders alike.[23] In a brilliant summary of the causes of the 1998 collapse of the Russian economy, Edward Luttwak remarks that 'young and inexperienced traders had only the vaguest ideas about the Russian economy – or anything else which did not appear on their computer screens'.[24] Pundits talk gravely of 'economic cycles' in which, at some point, capital retrenches following a period of over extension and then regroups to go on to better things. It is a sanguine view which fails to consider what Mészáros has described as 'the structurally incorrigible destructive tendencies of capital' evinced, not the least, in 'the contradiction of having to cripple the producer as the price to be paid for the success in reducing the material costs of production'.[25] It is not excessive to see a substantial part, if not all, of worldwide poverty as a consequence of that destructive process and, indeed, Marx has provided powerful arguments in support of such a view.[26] The problem that we are attempting to address in this book is that development theory and practice are simultaneously a response to the effects of capital and are conditioned by it. INGOs engaged either in development projects or in humanitarian assistance ignore or fudge this contradiction; liberal donor states categorise its discussion as 'political' and suggest that it is no business of development theorists, or at least of those that they fund.

Wahab's formulation of what development work should be about is unexceptionable but, if it is to be effective, then helping 'members of a society [to] develop themselves ... in ways that enhance their ability ... to produce sustainable and justly distributed improvements in their quality of life'[27] must mean enabling them to politicise. Politicisation, in turn, must be directed towards an inclusiveness which is actively undermined by the 'destructive tendencies of capital'. Over the last half century since the end of World War II and the subsequent formation of the Bretton Woods organisations, effectively protectionist institutions for US capital,[28] this contradiction has become increasingly apparent. So much so that substantial areas of development work have become merely palliative or have been replaced by minimalist welfare provision for the survivors of catastrophe. To palliate is not always and everywhere a bad thing, but it should not be confused with enabling a larger justice to prevail. Nor should it be supposed that where some project greater than the most minimal infrastructural improvement has been shown to survive, has been judged 'sustainable', it will not ultimately be subject to absorption into the larger and destructive priorities of market capitalism.

All this leads us to think again about the use of the word 'sustainable' and we have begun to do so by looking first at the ways in which our language works (Chapter 2) and the assumptions we make, often unconsciously, in theories about development. Developmental theorists, perhaps a little late in the day, have discovered the linguistic debate around post-modernism and, in some instances, have been seduced by its ideological relativism and, hence, its inability to deal with 'otherness'.[29] We cannot ignore important insights which have emerged as a consequence of that debate, but we will offer both a criticism of post-modern philosophical idealism and suggest an alternative to its cultural solipsism. It has been observed that environmental movements tend always to express their views in terms of sustainability[30] (in Chapter 3 we shall discuss this further), but, possibly because of the popularity of environmental issues, there is a distinct sense that when the word is used in other contexts it derives its primary meaning from ecological roots. In practice there are three principal groups of development analyses, each of which gives its own particular meaning to sustainability – the ecological, the economic and the socially just. Ecological sustainability is summed up in that memorable remark in the Brundtland Report[31] which called on the world at large to satisfy the needs of the present without compromising the resources available to future generations. We shall consider in Chapter 3 the effect on contemporary environmental thinking of the success, discussed in Chapter 2, of philosophical idealism and the consequent adoption of the agendas of the Enlightenment. We shall associate this with the development of the peculiarly environmental agenda of the UNCED held in Rio de Janeiro in June 1992 and look again at the reasons for it. We have already commented on economic sustainability, in Chapter 4 we shall discuss it more fully; it is a slippery concept, perhaps more so than either of the others since economics, like religion, tends to divide along parallel confessional lines which fail to meet, even in infinity. Richard Walker has neatly summarised a central strand in our argument:

> Accumulation is the main driving force of the world economy, along with its correlates, capital-capital competition and capital-labour exploitation. This is why it makes sense to speak of 'the capitalist system' rather than 'the global market'. The greatest economic myth of all is that the market has as its principal purpose the service of human needs rather than the aggrandisement of capitalists and their corporations.[32]

Chapter 5 will be devoted to our argument that socially just development, while it is not susceptible to simple description, must spring from certain principles which allow for the containment and rational direction of the other two. But 'social justice' is as polysemic as the two preceding categories and is equally compromised by the intellectual traditions which have informed the rest of the developed world. In our final chapter (Chapter 6) we shall offer some account of the challenges and limitations of historical and geographical interpretations of 'sustainable development' and compare what actually seems to be happening with what ought to be; a necessary discussion if only because poverty and its consequences are increasing.[33]

It should be obvious from the tone of this introduction that we have written a polemic, we do have an axe to grind. Our argument is simple enough: unless analyses of development begin not with the symptoms, environmental or economic instability, but with the cause, social injustice, then no development can be sustainable. We are arguing for a radical shift in the debate from concern with things to concern with societies, with people and their relationship to contemporary modes of production. No effective development or humanitarian work is possible without a grasp of its political nature, so we are also arguing for a complete reassessment of the ways in which we use the adjective 'sustainable'. The simplicities of its use in current debates within development theory and practice conceal catastrophic failures in political understanding and, hence, of political competence. We contend that political incompetence is unsustainable.

2
Polite Meaningless Words
(apologies to W.B. Yeats)

Ever since Noam Chomsky and Ferdinand de Saussure, in their very different ways, opened up new avenues for linguistic analysis, it has become commonplace to talk about 'discourse as power'. So much is this the case that some account of the ways in which we use language has become essential in any extended political discussion. Despite the complexity of the arguments which lie behind contemporary analyses of language, the issues are not, for general purposes, so difficult to follow. Discourse operates within linguistic structures, sets of meanings, which are largely formed by the society in which it is held. This is not to say that language and discourse are necessarily bound, or limited, by a cultural ossification, but merely that the dominant values of society are embodied in the linguistic and structural assumptions by which discourse proceeds. Where the exchange is between classes or between rich and poor states, the most powerful parties will do their utmost to ensure that it is their language, their values, which are seen as 'natural', as possessing 'sense' and as being obviously 'right', and when they are convincing it is usually because their apparent success has confirmed their own belief in the values that they advance. Success places them in hegemonic control of a situation, a society, a world in which it is unthinkable, because patently absurd, to challenge their values and their ends.

With this in mind we may consider John Gay[1] who famously observed that

> I know you lawyers can, with ease,
> Twist words and meanings as you please;
> That language, by your skill made pliant,
> Will bend to favour any client.

Like so many great satirists, his weapons were curious crosses between rapiers and bludgeons. Thus while, with considerable accuracy, he identified hypocrisy and double-dealing in the establishment of his time, discomfiting it sufficiently for it to ban the staging of *Polly*, his sequel to *The Beggar's Opera*, he preferred to smash it to the ground rather than attempt serious dissection and understanding. Those four are among the best remembered of his lines and it would be idle to impose contemporary political analyses on early eighteenth-century writing, but they do point to an abiding problem. Indeed, Gay's is a better example of the relationship between language and power than the one frequently taken from Lewis Carroll's *Through the Looking-Glass*. For Carroll, Humpty-Dumpty's view of words was a philosophical absurdity, lampooned even more effectively in the conversation about meaning between the March Hare and Alice in Chapter 7 of *Alice's Adventures in Wonderland*. Gay, on the other hand seems more clearly to recognise the hegemonic control of language exercised by the institutions of the ruling classes.

Carroll was defending what he understood as a common-sense view of language, that is to say that he recognised a grammar, no matter how nuanced, and meanings for words which were the products of some past and present social consensus which could be appealed to. Minor disputes about meaning could be settled by the academic lexicographers whose job is to record, usually some time after the event, the slow, glacial change in detail forced by common usage.[2] He was also engaged, particularly in the March Hare dialogue, in a polemical defence of the scholastic logic of Aristotle and of William of Ockham and he deals, among other things, with the notorious syllogistic mistake of the undistributed middle.[3] Discourse, in Carroll's world, was interpreted by the listener according to a commonly received canon. His was a classic view already under threat in his own day from the growing influence, even in Oxford, of Darwin.[4] But it took Nietzsche's revolution which, at the time, passed unnoticed by English academics, to vest the speaker, rather than the hearer, with the power to determine meaning:

The right of masters to confer names extends so far that one should allow oneself to grasp the origin of language itself as the expression of the power of the rulers.[5]

Colin McCabe, in his perceptive account of Saussure's achievement in linguistics, pointed to the heart of what many contemporary writers who have adopted Nietzsche's Dionysian and profoundly philological philosophy propose:

> In short there is no such entity as *langue* at the level of meaning. And indeed, strictly speaking, there is no such thing as meaning in so far as the term assumes an entity independent of the different ideological, political or theoretical conditions of utterance. It is not that a word has different meanings for different speakers but that the same lexical item appears in different discourses.[6]

We need only notice, in passing, the movement from the Nietzschean position to some forms of extreme post-structuralist relativism of which the most celebrated accounts are by Jacques Derrida and Jean-François Lyotard.[7]

If the post-structuralist argument is accepted uncritically, then it leads to a rigidly determinist account of the world in which exchanges between differing cultures and classes cannot be of understanding, but only of dominance. It does not reject otherness so much as render it irrelevant, because it is not susceptible to the categories imposed by capital's social conditioning – gender, class and ethnicity cannot be understood analytically for the same reason. Movement, in such a world, is reserved entirely to the powerful, to those who, in the Nietzschean sense, are able to name. Yet, despite its flaws, there is a substantial element of truth in the post-structuralist account, we do understand ourselves and the world at large in terms of the concepts, not only of our own society, but generally also of our own class. We may grasp this more easily if we generalise it in another form of discourse. Christians are anxious for us all to believe in the existence of God, so much so that in the flowering of Christian philosophy in the Middle Ages, much effort was devoted to finding proofs for her existence. The greatest of those philosophers, particularly using arguments around causality which are now widely criticised, proposed the thesis that God was necessary, but that knowledge of her and acceptance of her being depended on faith.[8] Since ecclesiastics had defined God as a supreme being greater than human understanding, the reason for abandoning argument in favour of faith is not hard to find. God can only communicate with us, if she does it at all, in human language, since, according to Christians, that is what she gave us. This means that all thought about God is anthropomorphic, we do not possess her language, whatever that may be. She is largely constructed in our own image and we can only interpret her in human concepts, something which remains true even if we were to believe in the special and private revelations said to be given to some saints. In this context we should recall Wittgenstein's memorable point that what cannot be communicated should be left unremarked.[9] To worship a being which, by constant theological assertion, is humanly incomprehensible inevitably calls for heroic belief in a variety of divine epiphanies which are entirely accessible in human terms.

Some of those advancing the thesis that reality is socially constructed adopt a strong version of the same principle. Just as the only language we have for God is human, so the only language we have for other societies, or 'nature', is that given to us by the dominant perceptions in our own society. We do not need to 'believe', as in the case of God, in other societies, nature or anything else to know that the phenomena we perceive and interpret exist, but we do need to recognise that our understanding depends on our significant organisation of what we perceive. Interpreting cognition is primarily a linguistic function, so the strong, or rigidly determinist, version of this argument reduces inter-communal, or inter-class, encounters to a matter of which is the most powerful. Arguments then frequently degenerate into assertions of culturally complex 'otherness' which deny understanding precisely because they are other. Class, gender and ethnicity are pushed out of consideration because they are all categories within that incomprehensible other – in its extreme forms post-structuralism is a rejection of politics and a surrender to power. The extent of that surrender may be gauged by the disappearance of poverty from political discourse and it is a surrender which we cannot permit.

It is, in general, a position arising from idealist philosophy, particularly German idealism flowing from Leibniz through, among others, Kant, Hegel and Dilthey. In one way or another all philo-sophical idealism, whether German or otherwise, begins its inquiry with individual perception and, as it were, moves outwards. In a real sense it is a psychologistic approach in which there is a hierarchy of perception which only allows society to be understood through its individual members. Understanding thus begins with an examina-tion of inner experience. Idealists reject the assumption that no intelligible account of inner experience or, indeed, of the inner self, may be given without reference to being-in-society or what Marx called 'species-being'. One of Marx's earliest references to this concept is to be found in his *Critique of Hegel's Philosophy of Right* (written in 1843)[10] in which he is simultaneously criticising Hegel's idealism and its consequent class politics.

A prescient argument against what later appeared as extreme post-structuralist relativism was produced by V.N. Vološinov in the Soviet Union of the late 1920s.[11] One crucial passage sums up the ground of his argument:

> If experience does have meaning and is not merely a particular piece of reality ... then surely experience could hardly come about other than in the material of signs. After all meaning can belong only to a sign; meaning outside a sign is a fiction. Meaning is the expression of a semiotic relationship between a particular piece of reality and another kind of reality that it stands for, represents, or depicts. Meaning is a function of the sign and is therefore incon-ceivable (since meaning is pure relation, or function) outside the sign as some particular, independently existing thing.[12]

In a preceding passage he has pointed to the fatal flaw in the idealist argument, to what he calls its 'proton pseudos', by remarking that 'they have no notion of the essential bond between meaning and sign, no notion of the specific nature of the sign'.[13] He had also remarked that for inner experience, for the operation of the 'subjec-tive human psyche', '*the reality of the inner psyche is the same reality of that of the sign*. Outside of the material of signs there is no psyche ...'.[14] Marx and Engels in their critique of Feuerbach made, for very different purposes, a similar point[15] and Wittgenstein approached it in another way in his account of ostensive definition.[16] Vološinov's analysis of the relationship of meaning and sign provides an elegant

foundation for the assertion that individuality and society are inseparable. Idealism, on the other hand, in its post-structuralist, relativist
incarnation treats all social interaction as transient epiphenomena
precisely because it ignores that 'bond between meaning and sign'; it
thus plunges us into political and philosophical quietism.

The relationship between meaning and sign is both intra- and
inter-communal. That is to say that no matter how extensively
powerful ruling elements in any given society have conditioned the
interpretation of concepts, even of words, in their own interests,
they are finally incapable of closing off alternatives. There are what
Wittgenstein called 'family likenesses' in the uses of language which
allow differences in comprehension between societies to be teased
out. For meaning to be given to absolute social and linguistic relativism it is necessary to postulate a language which is so solipsistic in
structure that it cannot permit dialectical development – a position
which is obviously historically absurd. A comprehensive refutation
of absolute relativism belongs elsewhere, here we need only recognise that post-structuralism, despite its hopelessly compromised
idealism, has given us at least one valuable insight. Nietzsche's association of discourse with power while not, as many
post-structuralists would maintain, an ultimate condition, is a social-
political reality with which we have to contend. This was
acknowledged in a significant passage in an essay by Lyotard: 'capitalism inherently possesses the power to derealise familiar objects,
social roles, and institutions to such a degree that the so-called real-
istic representations [in art] can no longer evoke reality except as
nostalgia or mockery'.[17] Lyotard's argument extends to all understanding and we shall have frequent cause to return to it as we
consider the political and social issues caught up in any discussion
or account of development.

Let us first look at one of the more important and insidious uses,
or abuses, of language in recent times. In any description, whether by
partisans or by critics, of *laissez-faire* capitalism and its pursuit of 'free'
markets, it is rare to read far without stumbling across the adjective
'liberal', sometimes with the puzzling prefix 'neo'. Thatcherite
economies are thus categorised, so, too, are the policies pursued by
the Bretton Woods institutions.[18] In trade, both national and international, the verb to 'liberalise' has come to mean the removal, so far
as possible, of any restraint on the labour and trading practices of the

TNCs. 'Free market' is used variously to mean the abandonment of national powers directly to protect indigenous production or consumption from foreign competition, and permission for the varying centres of capital power to compete unrestrainedly between themselves across any national borders. It has often been observed that such 'freedoms' are enjoyed only by the powerful marketeers and we may see these commandeerings of meaning as instances of capitalism's 'power to derealise familiar objects'.

Living languages, of course, change and develop, frequently as a consequence of the success of certain hegemonic discourses. As they do so, many words naturally occupy more than their original space and others may become obsolete and largely vanish. An example, particularly of the latter, may be seen in the battle, now virtually lost, over the difference between 'uninterested' and 'disinterested'. But that case was one of popular movement, no matter that we now seem not to have a word in the English language which conveys the earlier meaning of 'disinterested'. The current and widespread use of 'liberal' is different, it was commandeered to make a political point. If we adopt the techniques of Carroll's world, we discover that it is a word which, since its appearance in the written English language in the fourteenth century,[19] has, almost without exception, been used in a laudatory fashion. Oxford, in its third definition, lists only one exception – 'Free from restraint; free in speech or action. In 16th–17th c. often in a bad sense: Unrestrained by prudence or decorum, licentious.' – a use which has almost vanished from contemporary idiom. Nineteenth-century Tories could still use the word with the same venom that they subsequently invested in 'Communist' or 'left', thus Newman, complaining in a hand-wringing moment, wrote that 'schools of secular knowledge' could lead tender souls 'into a bottomless liberalism of thought'.[20] Nonetheless, liberality has customarily been thought to be virtuous and it was for this reason that the coalition, in the England of the 1860s, of moderate Whigs and Radicals in a reforming party, cheerfully took as its name the epithet 'liberal' with which its old Tory opponents, clinging to that seventeenth-century meaning, had berated them.

'Liberal' or 'neo-liberal' economic and political thinking has produced, in the industrialised world of the late twentieth century, the most illiberal of social conditions. In the name of 'liberalising' national economies it has reintroduced massive unemployment, it has increased social differences, undermined workers' organisations, made much employment 'flexible' – that is, underpaid and insecure – destroyed industries and their communities, and, above all, has driven millions of the already destitute in both industrialised and poor countries, into ever deeper and more insoluble poverty. In those countries describing themselves as 'democratic', power has shifted radically from states to the institutions of private capital, a process happily supported by the ruling classes, known more popularly as the 'fat-cats of the boardrooms'. Globalisation offers the poor, particularly those in the supposedly 'developing' countries, 'nothing but the perpetuation of the differential rate of exploitation'.[21] Using the word liberal to describe this process clearly emerges as 'an expression of power on the part of the rulers', and we are irresistibly reminded of the early twentieth-century argot in which the verb to 'liberate' meant to 'steal'.

It is no accident that 'liberal' was used in this fashion; the Thatcherite demotion of greed from its status as one of the seven deadly sins and the promotion of rampant individual accumulation demanded such window dressing. In his polemic, *False Dawn*,[22] a book engagingly rich in unsupported assertion, John Gray, by analysing the ways in which free trade is fundamentally at odds with democracy, incidentally illustrates the political purpose of this linguistic contortion – the making of discourse propagandising the otherwise untenable. Orwell, in *Animal Farm*, his satire on Stalinism, made the same point. But, in addition to making simple propaganda, the free-market ideologues of the Thatcher–Regan era were engaged not so much in thought policing, a sort of crisis management, as in a process of cultural absorption succinctly described, for other circumstances, by Paulo Freire:

> The very structure of their thought [that is, of the oppressed] has been conditioned by the contradictions of the concrete, existential situation by which they were shaped. Their ideal is to be men; but for them, to be a 'man' is to be an oppressor. This is their model of humanity.[23]

'Liberal' economic structures, like four legs, are good; state intervention, like two legs, is bad. Indeed, for the apologists of liberal economics, 'good' and 'bad' are not the right adjectives; 'natural' or 'necessary' are better than 'good', 'inconceivable' or 'insane' replace 'bad'. Opponents of this new liberalism are said not to be living in the real world. Exactly because discourse is power, language – meaning – as Freire, perhaps unconsciously following Vološinov, was at pains to point out, is as much an arena of class struggle as any other. Tony Blair's redefinition of the British Labour Party, his enthusiastic, if slightly shifty, embrace of most of Tory ideology entailing the exclusion of all but the most supine of trades unions, is an instance of this. In a succinct description of New Labour, Hurst and Thompson described it as substituting policy for principle and programmes for ideology, as opportunist and with no passion for righting injustice. They wrote of it as the party of managerial capitalism communicating by 'spin' and of the party which consciously abuses language by transforming people from being the motor of progress into more-or-less submissive clients.[24] Despite his triumphalism, Blair's managerial neo-liberalism will be recognised and, perhaps, ousted as surely as Thatcher's.

When grossly perverted usages become commonplace to the point where the recovery of less tendentious, or simply earlier, meanings calls either for extraordinary linguistic agility or for tedious explanation, then, obviously enough, we need to examine the extent to which they contaminate other discourses associated with them. Development, in its popular sense of enabling the poor to live decent human lives is, of course, one of them, though it might be more meaningful to see it as a web of discourses rather than in the singular. Its language is notoriously problematic, not the least because of the reluctance of many of its participants to define their terms. Nonetheless, there is a general assumption throughout the industrialised world (Mészáros remarks that 'industrial', in this context, is a euphemism for 'capitalist'[25]), that the purpose of development, particularly overseas, is to raise standards of living for the poor and to give them access to 'resources' sufficient to allow them to compete effectively in the world's markets – somehow, as the cant phrase has it, 'to bring them into the present century'.

What is generally evaded in this scheme of things is that the model for development, no matter how distantly, is related to the concept of industrialised, that is capitalist, social democracy; the middle-class comfort, with all its trappings, of the capitalist world becomes the standard of achievement, no matter how far in the future, for 'developing societies'. This is rarely directly articulated and is subsumed under vague discourse about reducing the glaring gaps in income between the richest 10 per cent and the poorest 10 per cent of the world's population. The poorest 10 per cent are frequently said to be socially excluded,[26] but the society from which they are kept out is generally one in which the physical gains, at least, are measured in terms of bourgeois culture and capitalist consumerism. Those of us concerned with the injustices of global poverty not uncommonly refer to the famous 'eighty-twenty' division: 80 per cent of the world's resources are controlled and consumed by 20 per cent of the world's population. Global markets, global institutions of finance, giant corporations and so on form, control and depend on the capital structures which buttress this inequitable division and it is increasingly the case that those standards of living we either cherish or to which we aspire are also dependent on it. To suggest that somehow, by the processes of development, most, or even a substantial proportion, of the 80 per cent of the people of the world controlling only 20 per cent of its resources can be brought, more or less, to enjoy the cultural and consumerist fruits of a well-managed, advanced and just capitalism is plainly absurd. Yet the problem is precisely that the poor are unable to consume enough.[27]

   This excursion into the obvious points up the ways in which the words we use in this context are, at best, uncertain, and, at worst, positively absorbed into the agendas of capital. We may, with profit, briefly consider another treacherous area: in recent years, only slightly antedating the transformation of, for example, those travelling by rail in Britain from passengers to customers, we have become accustomed to thinking of many of our working relationships as operating in the 'market-place'. Even without bringing into the discussion essential Marxian concepts like the exploitation of labour, the extraction of surplus value and alienation, we may see in this shift some curious delusions. Implied in the use of this phrase is a mixture of macho posturing (we can *sell* our labour, *drive* a good bargain) and a belief that this ill-defined 'market' will, in some way, put matters in order. It depends on that greatest of all capitalist illusions, that the 'market' is an independent reality which will settle relationships equitably and, despite occasional hiccoughs, will always correct any distortions within itself which might lead to unreasonable levels of social exclusion. It does this by finding the optimal price for everything, 'optimal' meaning the price at which most of what is at issue can be sold and a profit made. For the few unable to capitalise their labour sufficiently to afford necessities priced in this way, some state support, paid for out of minimal taxation, may be countenanced. Even economists and commentators noted chiefly for their desire to reform rather than to dismantle capitalism, have frequently attacked this *ignis fatuus*[28] though some have been deluded by it.[29] 'Market' is, of course, another of those words which conjures up reassuring, even romantic, images. In this it is deeply misleading, not the least because it does not exist as a 'place', but as a set of relationships dictated by fierce competition regulated only in the interests of the major competitors.

All this is very familiar territory, but it is important to remind ourselves of the minefield lurking in our discourses and we shall have occasion frequently to return to the issues. Language has been perverted to suit the political agenda of the so-called 'new right' (its novelty seems open to doubt) and it is worth recalling just why that agenda was formulated. Capital in its globalising phase has demanded not only a diminution in the role of national borders, but also the transfer of much fiscal sovereignty from states to those institutions of governance designed to facilitate the programme of the TNCs. The European Union, in its previous incarnations first as a customs and trading union, and then as the European Community, was created as a bloc partly to end disastrous rivalry between France and Germany and then to confront the increasing trading power of US and Japanese capital.[30] We have become familiar, in the course of its development into much more than a simple customs union, with the growing absorption of many of the functions previously belonging to individual states into the EU's instruments of governance. Agricultural policy under the Common Agricultural Policy (CAP), interest rates determined by the Central Bank (even, to a considerable degree, for those countries like Britain refusing, at least for the time being, to opt for the single currency), the setting of common tariffs, subsidies and many conditions of sale and so on are all examples. Another instance of such a union may be seen in the now seriously frayed NAFTA. Similar, world-wide, processes are at work as the WTO, instituted by the Uruguay Round of the General Agreement on Tariffs and Trade (GATT) which ended with its

Marrakesh Declaration of April 1994, and which acts as a supervisory body, with substantial legal powers, ensures that nation states, or groups of them, do not erect 'unfair' barriers to free trade. More recently the OECD's furtive production of the MAI,[31] even though it was abandoned following disagreements among the more economically powerful states,[32] would, if it is ever generally ratified (it was subsequently resuscitated by the WTO, see Chapter 4), add enormously to the process. Since between 70 and 80 per cent of all world trade lies in the hands of the TNCs, this centralisation of power is effectively clearing space for the greater efficiency of capital.

Capitalism is said to 'work', it is credited, by its protagonists, with delivering higher standards of living for people in its core countries and, until recently, of giving birth to economic wonders it calls 'tigers'. Its apologists boast that the rate of progress is such that, at some uncertain date in the near future, most of the world will share in similar new dawns. We became aware of the fragility of these tiger-cubs as their economies in South East Asia collapsed[33] and the seriously partitioned 'Celtic tiger', the sole northern specimen, reveals both its fiscal corruption[34] and its dependence on the vagaries of TNC investment. Of course it is true that technologies, mainly driven by capital, which do enhance the lives of those with access to them now exist and that many more people live in comfort, and live longer, than at any time in the past. But capitalism has plainly not worked, since the numbers absolutely excluded from its benefits are even more enormous (1.5 billion according to the World Bank) and are growing. Countless millions of others who 'share' only peripherally in the benefits of the system fight daily to avoid absolute exclusion. Here it is perhaps important to make clear that these remarks apply just as surely to the now defunct state capitalism of Stalin's USSR as they do to the globalised capitalism of the TNCs and the banks – the word 'socialist' was misappropriated by the successors to the October Revolution. State capitalism 'derealises' as surely as any other form of capitalism.

The system is, unsurprisingly, both selective and fickle. Few people now take seriously its favourite nostrum, that increased investment in poorer economies will, by a process of 'trickle down', gradually raise everyone's condition. Investors, like sheep, follow one another, they put their money only in those places which they collectively identify as viable markets or as 'efficient', that is cheap, regions for production. This has meant that the greater part of investment in the developing world has been concentrated on 'a core group of about a dozen countries in Asia and Latin America'.[35] So it is, for example, that although about 12 per cent of the world's population lives in Sub-Saharan Africa, its share of both trade and investment is approximately only 1 per cent of the world's total,[36] a proportion which exposes the absurdity of the expression 'trickle down'. Fickleness accompanies this selectivity; the collapse of the South East Asian economies, particularly since the end of 1997, was generated largely by heated speculation on the international financial markets and marginally added to by the corruption of ruling élites. Indonesia, Malaysia, the Philippines, South Korea and Thailand have all suffered from the massive retreat of capital, but most other poor countries will also be affected by that collapse as investors class them all together. The IMF, in rushing to the rescue of these ailing economies, while ignoring desperately poor countries, has produced its usual recipes which include huge cuts in spending in the already minimal welfare provision for the poorest sectors in the 'tiger' states. All the evidence suggests that the Fund has an unblemished record of complete failure in its dramatic rescue attempts.[37] It is, of course, true that the general panic has threatened the ill-organised and cumbersome financial giants of Japan and, if it were to occur, their collapse could spread to the remainder of the capitalist world. Russia, even despite a fundamentally strong economy, has hovered over the brink of fiscal ruin, though its main difficulty, by the end of 1998, was not economic but political – its state seemed close to collapse, diverted only by the renewal of the Chechen war. It hardly needs pointing out that those who will suffer most in the capitalist world will also chiefly be the poor.

Reasons for this failure are not hard to find. Capitalism is a competitive system whose institutions – corporations, companies and banks – depend for their survival on exploiting the surplus value generated by the labour of others. Based on some principle of competitive accumulation, the institutions and the system itself survive only so long as they can expand, and the measure of expansion is an increase in the value of institutional capital. Competition between institutions is familiar as they fight to dominate what they see as their markets, co-existence only happens when the market is thought to be large enough, but taking over or destroying competitors is fairly normal. Reducing costs in order to maximise profit is proof of real virtue, hence the need always to contain workforces. Organised labour is understood as a threat to the efficient operation of the market, which is why, in Britain, Thatcher set about wrecking the trades unions and why her epigones in New Labour are cheerfully cantering down the same course.[38] Throughout the history of capitalism, combination has been opposed; individuals can be set into competition with one another and persuaded that they are 'marketing' their labour to make money in much the same sense that, for example, Nestlé sells synthetic milk to adequately lactating mothers whose babies would generally do better without it. Isolated and insecure workers are biddable; where some company loyalty is necessary, then workers' councils set up within corporations, sometimes backed by bribes in the form of small share options, are obviously easier to control. Individual workers are thus persuaded into the ethos of capitalism, persuaded by some caricature of Darwinism that competition for everything, including work (there is no 'right' to work in this system) is natural.

Labour in the capitalist world, in its long battle to create protective organisations, has principally achieved victories in those moments when capital was most in need of it, that is, when production and new investment were increasing. This was particularly the case in the beginning of the second half of the twentieth century following World War II. As capital's need for labour decreased towards the end of that period, which means as capital itself weakened, its social-democratic governments have recovered the territory, destroyed unions, replaced them with intra-company workers' councils or have drawn their teeth in partnership agreements of the kind found in Germany and Ireland. Capital can only absorb – what it cannot digest it can only reject and treat as inimical, eventually, in some sense, as *unlawful*. Anti-union legislation is one obvious example, but so, too, is the automatic labelling of any resistance to capital's puppet regimes in poor countries as 'terrorist'. Mészáros describes this as 'Capital's Order of Metabolic Reproduction'[39] which results in 'an *ultimately uncontrollable mode of social metabolic control*'.[40] National social democracies have served global capital well in transferring many of their most important economic powers to the WTO and in creating that 'flexible' workforce. Both these moves will increasingly enable capital to override any indigenous control of resources or production which might begin to contain the TNCs, particularly in the poorest regions of the world, and, by rendering labour defenceless and only dealing with workers individually, have prevented the resurgence of traditional labour movements of opposition. The unaccountability of global TNC capital is thus demonstrably anti-democratic – a condition manifested just as clearly in the increasingly unaccountable global institutions of governance which are rapidly eroding the powers of the more or less democratically elected governments of existing states.

It is not difficult to see why those controlling this monstrous structure must tinker with our consciousness by means of an extensive renaming; as an example we may consider the degree to which right-wing social-democratic parties, like the present British Labour Party, call themselves parties of the centre. This chapter has been largely devoted to explaining why this is not mere sleight of hand, but underwrites a discourse of power. Our argument about the use of language has been set out in skeletal form because it is not our principal thesis, it was intended simply to draw attention to what are often barely conscious assumptions – the agendas concealed by uncritical uses of specific professional discourses. It is here that we must turn to one of the most significant of terms within development discourse – 'sustainable development'. To a certain extent the adjective needs rescue because, like so many other high-sounding words, it is often used to conceal a disagreeable reality. Casualties in a war may be 'sustainable', usually concealing the fact that too many people were killed for the actual number to be announced, either for fear of comforting the enemy or of discouraging the survivors. Company financial losses may be 'sustainable', meaning that it is not quite time to call in the receivers but investors should not expect much return. That a workforce must be rendered sustainable usually means that numbers of workers will lose their livelihoods – no doubt plenty of other dubious or risible examples will spring to the reader's mind. For our purposes it is enough to observe that in development discourse the word is shrouded in confusion, not the least because of the failure, mentioned in the last chapter, of the Brundtland Commission to define it. But it is confused largely because it has come to be used as the final and clinching assertion in any argument for a particular course of action and so many courses of action in development have proved to be mutually incompatible. In the succeeding chapters we will look at the ways in which the word is used by theorists and practitioners in development and at some of the principal agendas these uses conceal.

3
All Nature Is But Art
(Pope, *An Essay on Man*)

Our remarks on discourse as power bear heavily on any discussion of the meaning and practice of environmentally sustainable development. Because, as we observed in the last chapter, our ways of seeing are formed historically within the dominant culture of our own society and are imprinted with its values and understanding, there is a sense, not wholly to be dismissed, that social reality is constructed.[1] Social reality must include whatever is meant by 'nature' although there is no nature 'out there' of which we are not a part and which is not mediated through our own consciousness including, of course, our ideologies. All reality is mediated by our perceptions, themselves heavily compromised or conditioned by our mores. Into this recognition we must insert that other truism that no meaning can attach to any attempt to give primacy either to the individual or to society – an exercise, as E.H. Carr pointed out, redolent of the riddle about the chicken and the egg.[2]

Our remarks apply to all three of our groups of uses of 'sustainable' (environmental, economic and socially just), but they are particularly germane to any consideration of the 'natural' environment. The issues become more tractable once we recognise that our experience of the multiplicity of phenomena put loosely under the heading 'nature' has long been an emotional and political battleground. For many it has replaced poverty as a matter of concern and animals, even ecosystems and their constituent elements, begin to be endowed with 'rights' which are worthy of protection.[3] This view is a late creation of romanticism, a philosophy which owes its origin, according to the English philosopher Anthony Quinton, to Kant's 'distinction between reason and understanding'.[4] The present authors feel that Rousseau's supposition that the further humanity got from a 'state of nature' the more corrupt it became, although formulated with a different objective, may also have played its part.[5] It is a categorical division mimetic of, indeed inspired by, the individualistic psychologism of idealist philosophy; Hegel saw this division as a major intellectual and aesthetic advance because it accords 'with what Christianity asserts of God as spirit'.[6]

William Wordsworth was one of the greatest influences in the rise of romanticism in English culture. He was inspired by the Enlightenment ideology of the French Revolution and, before his mid-life lurch to the right, married that, a little uneasily, with an upper-class view of the countryside inherited from the eighteenth century. A passage taken from 'Lines composed a few miles above Tintern Abbey' sums up what, right up until the present day, is a common reaction to nature throughout the capitalist world:

> For I have learned
> To look on nature, not as in the hour
> Of thoughtless youth; but hearing oftentimes
> The still, sad music of humanity,
> Nor harsh nor grating, though of ample power
> To chasten and subdue. And I have felt
> A presence which disturbs me with the joy
> Of elevated thoughts; a sense sublime
> Of something far more deeply interfused,
> Whose dwelling is the light of setting suns,
> And the round ocean and the living air,
> And the blue sky, and in the mind of man.

It is significant that Wordsworth, 'A worshipper of Nature', dispenses with the divine as an explanation and, instead, links his 'joy of elevated thoughts' with the reassurance he offers to his sister that in any future, no matter how dark, she will have this remembrance of times past. The ruins of Tintern, like Caspar David Friedrich's celestial Harz mountains seen through the eyes of his ecstatic, conservative bourgeois self,[7] become the place in which God is replaced by a humanistic romanticism. This poem is among the most powerful examples of the *ideological* production of nature expressed, not as nature's absorption into capital's modes of production, but as an intellectual instrumentality which permits of that process.

Romanticism itself is a complex philosophy not easily amenable to definition and more easily understood as a coherent cluster of attitudes. Among the most important of these, for our purposes, is the tendency to search for the 'sense sublime' in the particular reality and to find justification for it. Vološinov saw romanticism as a 'reaction against the last resurgences of the cultural power of the alien world – the epochs of the Renaissance and neoclassicism'.[8] What it certainly did was to influence for generations the ways in which nature was understood in the capitalist world, resulting in a quasi-pantheist account in which the 'natural' world is both property and a source of inspiration – a view which substantially informs, for example, much of the thinking about 'environmental degradation'.

James Lovelock, a far from disreputable successor to the romantic tradition, has been particularly influential. In his popular and seminal work *Gaia*[9] he gave one of the most compelling contemporary accounts of the interrelatedness of virtually everything. Many authors have popularised the understanding of 'ecosystems' and we are all familiar with the pitfalls of thinking of phenomena of any kind in isolation from the 'systems' which sustain them and are sustained by them. We know, too, that this perception is not confined simply to individuals within systems, but extends to relationships between systems. That these views have advanced both scientific exploration and engendered a more sophisticated popular appreciation of the world we inhabit is beyond question and much of this change may be attributed to Lovelock's scientifically based and inspirational work. Running through it, however, is his gentle but insistent advancement of what he calls 'the Gaia hypothesis'. He introduces it 'as a complex entity involving the Earth's biosphere, atmosphere, oceans, and soil; the totality constituting a feedback or cybernetic system which seeks an optimal physical and chemical environment for life on this planet. The maintenance of relatively constant conditions by active control may be conveniently described by the term "homeostasis".'[10]

We may quibble with his use of the word 'entity' since it seems to confer ostensive reality on what is actually a cognitive act, but the more important form of the problem is raised in the next paragraph where this 'entity' abruptly becomes 'she'. Lovelock had come to the name of his system with the help of the novelist William Golding, it is one of the names of Mother Earth in the Olympian creation myths and he remarks that:

> The Gaia of this book is a hypothesis but, like other useful hypotheses, *she* has already proved *her* theoretical value, if not *her* existence, by giving rise to experimental questions and answers which were profitable exercises in themselves.[11]

By the end of the book the hypothetical nature of Lovelock's structure has retreated a little to be replaced, admittedly as much for brevity as for any other reason, by phrases like 'a key Gaian process' (113), 'Living with Gaia' (the title of Chapter 8) and 'Gaia has vital organs at the core' (119). All this seems suspiciously like anthropomorphism and while Lovelock has obviously found it useful as a means of seeing things differently, it is perfectly possible to accept much of his argument about the essential interconnectedness of things without the need to follow him in thinking about it in this quasi-deistic fashion.

Gaia is a late romantic concept incorporating Wordsworth's 'sense sublime of something far more deeply interfused'. Nonetheless it is also a concept which has informed another strand in twentieth-century environmental thinking, that which Martin W. Lewis describes as eco-radicalism or deep ecology. So far as we are aware, Lovelock is not a deep ecologist in any political sense yet, if Lewis is right in his assertion that '[d]eep ecologists ... regard nature as forming an interconnected totality, the whole of which is much greater than the sum of its parts',[12] then there is substantial sympathy between them. Lewis distinguishes five main groups of eco-radicals[13] and remarks that advocates for three of them (he has slightly more sympathy for eco-Marxism and eco-feminism) argue for an 'ecological justice' in which all natural phenomena, systems as well as species (in some versions, only those which are not human), are recognised as independent and intrinsically valuable beings. Human beings are simply another species and must not only respect but in no way disturb ecological balance and its relationships or, at worst, disturb them very little. There are gradations in the totality of this position; some less comprehensive deep ecologists demand justice only for all sentient creatures and their ecologies, others restrict it even further to the higher animals. In much deep ecology we can detect the influence of Thoreau, particularly if we consult the final paragraph of 'The Ponds' chapter in *Walden*.[14] Engagement in this argument belongs elsewhere[15] and we are only concerned with it as one influence in the current environmental debate; but, in passing, we should note that it, too, is philosophically grounded in the German idealism which also lies behind post-structural *angst*.[16] We are only drawing attention to deep ecology, at least in the first three forms described by Lewis, as one strand among several which have formed the consciousness of the capitalist world in its political and economic confrontations with the impoverished. It is necessary to remind ourselves that the pace of discovery in much contemporary natural science is compelling the formation of new political analyses by some of its practitioners, no matter how influenced by late romanticism they may have been. This has been made apparent in an accessible way by the work of writers like Stephen Jay Gould.

It is commonplace, at least within the urban world of capitalism, that people do not see themselves as part of nature even though the phrase 'human nature' occurs in everyday speech. If pressed, it is probable that few would deny that 'nature' must, as a category, include humanity, but in practice the majority mean by the word all living things other than people and, possibly, their domestic pets, which are 'there' to be exploited for human good. For much of the first half of the twentieth century, concern in the capitalist world about the 'goods' of nature largely revolved around agricultural and fishery prices and, particularly following World War I, opening up privatised and enclosed land for recreational purposes. In many countries, especially England, access to the latter formed a small, but significant, part of the struggle for working-class emancipation. Not until the 1960s were recalcitrant landlords replaced in the public eye as the principal environmental monsters by the evils of industrial pollution. They were, nevertheless, swiftly restored to a joint position with industrialists when popular understanding caught up with agriculture as an industry every bit as polluting as the more familiar factories. Public consciousness of pollution was also increased by the creation of the nuclear power industry as a by-product of nuclear weaponry – nuclear blast and its fall-out might pollute us all to death and it does seem an extraordinary way to boil water. The subsequent rise of environmental activism, often as an alternative to apparently sterile party politics, was rapid and is now a major force to be reckoned with in the 'developed' world.

People have always been excited by apocalypse and, in 1962, Rachel Carson's *Silent Spring* reached an appreciative, if somewhat alarmed, audience.[17] In 1971, the Club of Rome uttered awful warnings, particularly about what it saw as a potentially catastrophic rise in world population, by which, of course, it meant among the poor. During the 1970s Barbara Ward wrote three hugely influential books, of which the most important, *Only One Earth* written with René Dubos, substantially broadened the popular base of environmentalism.[18] Widespread public pressure led to the establishment, by the United Nations, of the Conference on the Human Environment, held in Stockholm in 1972 which, in turn, was succeeded by the WCED (1983–85), chaired by Gro Harlem Brundtland. To a considerable degree the Brundtland Report, issued by the WCED, set the contemporary public environmental agenda and pushed the UN into the subsequent Conference on Environment and Development. The present writers have discussed Brundtland and the UNCED at length elsewhere,[19] but we must briefly revisit them.

During her rise in Norwegian politics, Gro Harlem Brundtland had spent a substantial term as Minister of the Environment and that background was used by the Secretary-General of the UN to persuade her to accept the chair of the WCED.[20] This is significant because it underlines the fundamentally environmentalistic origins of the report and, hence, of the subsequent conference. We should also note that the most prominent movers in the environmental movement up until, and including, the formation of the WCED, were women. The slightly dubious proposition that this is because women are in some way more sympathetic to the issues should, we think, be set against the possibility that powerful men took no leading part because they failed to recognise the political importance of the environmental movement; once they did so they tried to take over the initiative. The goals of the WCED, under the rubric of 'A global agenda for change' were:

- to propose long-term environmental strategies for achieving sustainable development by the year 2000 and beyond;

- to recommend ways [in which] concern for the environment may be translated into greater cooperation among developing countries and between countries at different stages of economic and social development ... [taking] account of the interrelationships between people, resources, environment, and development;
- to consider ways and means by which the international community can deal more effectively with environmental concerns.[21]

The final clause in this charge, which we have not quoted, is an elaboration of the others. At no point was it ever in doubt that the principal concern of the WCED was the worldwide resolution of what was primarily, even peculiarly, an issue for the capitalist world. Industrial pollution and industrially generated environmental degradation, in all their myriad forms, are grave threats to human life and health and to innumerable ecosystems. Environmental damage will further impoverish the already poor and add to the destitution, frequently the starvation, of countless thousands. The problem, however, has been produced, in the main, by capitalist industry, a fact recognised, though with some demurrals in the direction of the Third World, in the Brundtland Report.[22]

The WCED strove mightily to direct their enquiries and conclusions towards the needs of people, both those currently living in dire poverty and those to come in future generations, but it was a lost cause. Not only was the Commission's brief fundamentally environmental and, therefore, largely to do with the problems of capital, but its legal proposals also began with a curiously narrow account of 'Fundamental Human Right': 'All Human beings have the fundamental right to an environment adequate for their health and well-being.'[23] Of course, it may be argued quite correctly that 'an environment adequate for their health and well-being' must imply a reasonable degree of freedom from dire poverty, but it is at least an oddity to cast this first in an environmental form. Article 25 of the *Universal Declaration of Human Rights* is more direct:

Everyone has the right to a standard of living adequate for the health and well-being of himself [*sic*] and of his [*sic*] family, including food, clothing, housing and medical care and necessary social services, and the right to security in the event of unemployment, sickness, disability, widowhood, or old age or other lack of livelihood in circumstances beyond his [*sic*] control.

This right is reiterated in clause 14 of the 1993 Vienna Declaration of the UN World Conference on Human Rights, even though it is cast as a weak plea for everyone to try harder.

The UNCED, also known variously as 'Rio' or the 'Earth Summit', was convened, five years later, specifically to examine the world's progress in the issues raised by the Brundtland Report. In mediating the discussion of poverty through environmental problems, the Report had already reduced what the capitalist powers, chiefly the USA, saw as both political and economic threats posed by confronting poverty directly, to a less easily defined and apparently less contentious field. This was not enough, the US and its allies set about the complete emasculation of the Conference's agenda, almost wrecking it in advance. Those powerful men had woken up to the dangers of environmentalism and set about neutralising it. When, at last, it took place it produced some predictably damp squibs – conventions on biodiversity and climate, a statement of intent on forests and the *Rio Declaration on Environment and Development*; it also adopted the aspirational, but toothless, *Agenda 21*. President Bush's subsequent refusal to accept the Framework Convention on Biodiversity rendered even this milk-and-water result from the 'Summit to Save the World' nugatory.[24] The capitalist powers had brought off a sleight of hand by largely removing not only poverty from the Rio agenda, but even removing people from it. All the agreements and major statements are to do with phenomena which, while they affect everyone, are phenomena in nature – these were agreements about things and not about people. More positively, *Agenda 21*, despite its lack of specific heads of agreement and lack of any legal force, has become a focus for much local quasi-political activity, particularly in the industrialised world. It would be curmudgeonly to deny its value, but it, too, is compromised by aims more to do with fears in the developed world than with the needs of the absolutely poor. It suffers from other difficulties: a recent collection of reports on the progress of *Local Agenda 21* in several north European states suggests that it has been inhibited by a lack of agreement about the meaning of 'sustainable development'.[25]

There was a yet more disagreeable element in this shift in concern from people to environment since it had been based, following Schumacher and others, on a neo-Malthusian account of the world as a sort of spaceship with a strictly finite carrying capacity. Maurice Strong, Secretary-General of the UNCED, in opening the Conference, suggested 'that overpopulation in the South and overconsumption in the North were root causes of environmental degradation'.[26] The World Bank, publishing shortly after the Rio summit, wrote, in the 'Overview' of its annual development report, of reducing poverty by means of environmental improvement.[27] In a sub-section entitled 'The importance of population and poverty programmes' it details the extent to which the world's poorest are to blame for their own and, to a considerable degree, our predicament.[28] It is an elision comparable with that in the UNCED itself: people in the capitalist world may consume too much, but those who live in poor countries are destroying their environment and, by derivation, ours in their eagerness to develop. They do this because there are so many of them and resources are scarce. In both the UNCED and the World Bank's report, the victim thus becomes the problem.

The *UN Framework Convention on Climate Change* (UNFCCC), usually called 'the Climate Convention', was another purely aspirational document produced by the UNCED. It lacked not only teeth, but any serious proposals for addressing the problems that many scientists saw as springing from increases in global temperatures added to by human intervention. But the UNFCCC was an international agreement to attempt to stabilise greenhouse gas concentrations in the atmosphere in order to reduce human interference with the climate – it led to the Conference of the Parties of the Climate Change Convention in Kyoto (December, 1997). Its purpose was to deal, belatedly, with the catastrophic climatic effects of industrial and transport emissions. Car manufacturers and the oil companies had formed a profoundly destructive organisation, nauseatingly entitled the Global Climate Coalition, which had been remarkably successful in persuading the US government to prevent the UNCED from adopting anything more serious that the UNFCCC. Both in Rio and in Kyoto it set out to subvert the effects of scientific evidence for climate change consequent on the escalating production of greenhouse gases. It spent a fortune importuning, propagandising and entertaining delegates to persuade them into refusing, postponing or minimising emission targets. Minimalist targets were adopted and some governments of industrialised countries have even, marginally, improved on them. But the world's worst polluter, the US, having accepted derisory targets, abandoned even these as a consequence of domestic pressure brought to bear on the US Senate by the Coalition and its Republican allies. Since then the US has refused to move on the issue, but, since the Coalition seems to be fraying, it is possible that, at some point in the future, it may compromise a little.[29]

Environmentalism suffers from another conceptual difficulty – it tends primarily to be concerned with the rural world except when it considers the effects of industry and transport. Einstein, clearly a German idealist at heart, dealing with the matter more effectively, is said to have remarked that 'the environment is everything that isn't me',[30] and, as a general proposition, it is true. A false distinction is commonly made in the use of the phrase 'natural environment', it usually refers to everything not manufactured – a use which glides over the extent to which the world's landscapes have been modified by human activity. It misses, too, the extent to which that activity and the consequent changes in nature accurately reflect changing modes of production – contemporary nature is produced by capitalism. Humanity is also nothing if not part of nature; in that sense our built environment is as natural as the nest of the bird and its artefacts are as natural as the beaver's dam. David Harvey, in his extraordinary, sometimes politically and philosophically contentious, book *Justice, Nature and the Geography of Difference*,[31] gives an excellent account of cities as 'created ecosystems' and remarks:

> Human beings, like all other organisms, are 'active *subjects* transforming nature according to its laws' and are always in the course of adapting to the ecosystems they themselves construct. It is fundamentally mistaken, therefore, to speak of the impact of society *on* the ecosystem as if these two are separate systems in interaction with each other.[32]

Harvey is referring here to a point he has already made, that, for example, 'New York City [is] a "created ecosystem".'[33] This is a view which may not transform the environmentalist agenda but which should, at least, cause its modification, since it undermines the tendency to distinguish between 'nature' and the presumably 'unnatural' constructs of humanity. We feel that it actually renders the distinction, if not meaningless, then unusable and, as a consequence, forces the discussion to change direction. What it also subverts is the common acceptance of environmental issues as primarily to do with the simple evaluation of the environment as provider of 'goods' supporting human activity.[34] Given the tortuousness of some of Harvey's argument, it may be necessary to make the obvious point that he is in no way denying that people are perfectly capable of ruining their own environments.

Lying behind this is the difficulty of establishing an intellectual framework, a mathesis (to borrow Foucault's use of the word), from which to analyse the nature of environmental issues. Harvey sets out this problem very concisely at the end of the 'Prologue' to Part II of his book. He points out that among environmentalists in general the issues are confined to fairly specific areas:

> primarily focusing on the relationship between human activity and well-being ... and (a) the condition or 'health' of the biome or ecosystem which supports human life, (b) specific qualities of air, water, soil, and landscapes, and (c) the quantities and qualities of the 'natural resource base' for human activity.[35]

This is about a managerial approach to the environment and so implies a particular ideological stance in the very questions which are raised, but it is a stance which goes largely unexamined by those who raise them. Not only, as Harvey observes, does this position contain an unsupported but 'implicit division between "nature" and "culture"', it reinforces the 'long-standing distinction between the country and the city'. Part II of *Justice, Nature and the Geography of Difference* is devoted to creating a suitable mathesis, not dominated by an idealist approach, from which to discuss the environment and, perhaps even more importantly, to determine what the issues are.[36] Much the same point about the relationship between culture and environment is made by Susana Narotzky when she asserts that 'the environment is *always* the product of social historical processes'.[37]

The present authors feel that Harvey's insistence that all the major issues are, in effect, part of the class struggle or subject to a class analysis is substantial and convincing, and that his defence of urban society as another ecosystem is excellent; he offers many other joys. We are, however, in profound disagreement with him in his new account of class and with his failure to consider contemporary Marxist thinking about the nature of capital and accumulation. Further, and even greater, disagreement arises over Harvey's interpretation of German idealism: his concentration on Leibniz rather than Hegel (since Marx was clearly responding to the latter)[38] allows him to evade many central class issues. Indeed, it is not until fairly late in his book that he proposes a redefinition of class as 'situatedness or positionality in relation to processes of capital accumulation'.[39] This is, obviously, a reductionist position and, we feel, owes more to his private *angst* about contributing to a pension fund than to the realities of class conflict in late, *laissez-faire* capitalism. His account of urban life as ecosystems is admirable, but, possibly because of his redefinition, he does not pay much attention to what might add up to, or even replace, proletarian class struggle within them. Neither does he discuss the way in which Marx constructed his own dialectics as a methodical undermining of idealism. We are also in disagreement with him over his understanding of Raymond Williams's 'militant particularisms'. Nonetheless, these disagreements cannot take away from the importance of Harvey's adventurous and innovative work.

Harvey's position derives from Marxism, in particular from a late Marxist philosophy of language, and his argument relies on supplanting the psychologism of idealist thinking with dialectics; transformation, understood dialectically, is mutual – we are part of, create and change ecosystems and are, in turn, recreated, changed and absorbed by them. What such a view does in undermining the alienation of the environment as human 'property' is fundamentally to challenge many of the existing environmental agendas. Obviously enough, it is also, if accepted, a mortal blow to the romanticism of the deep ecologists. For our purposes it becomes the starting point for an attack on the tendency of the economically powerful to see the environment both as commodity and as a diversion from the real issues of poverty. It also qualifies, to a substantial degree, whatever might be meant by 'environmental sustainability'. Escobar points to the incorrigible tendency among the development and conservation agencies of the industrialised world to refer to 'ecological capital',[40] a tendency reinforced several years ago in the Brundtland Report[41] and which became one of the ideological planks in the UNCED's *Framework Convention on Biodiversity*, the phrasing of which is curiously revealing; two quotations from it will illustrate the point. In the manner of all such agreements, the signatories, in the preamble to the Convention, 'recognise'

> the close and traditional dependence of many indigenous and local communities embodying traditional lifestyles on biological resources, and the desirability of sharing equitably benefits arising from the use of traditional knowledge, innovations and practices relevant to the conservation of biological diversity and the sustainable use of its components.

In Article 8, entitled *In-situ Conservation*, they agree that each contracting party shall

> [s]ubject to its national legislation, respect, preserve and maintain knowledge, innovations and practices of indigenous and local communities embodying traditional lifestyles relevant for the conservation and sustainable use of biological diversity and promote their wider application with the approval and involvement of the holders of such knowledge, innovations and practices and encourage the equitable sharing of the benefits arising from the utilization of such knowledge, innovations and practices.

Escobar remarks that 'ethnic and peasant communities in the tropical rain-forest areas of the world are finally being recognized as owners of their territories (or what is left of them) but only to the extent that they accept to treat it – and themselves – as reservoirs of capital'.[42] The Framework Convention committed no one to very much, but it did reinforce the legitimacy of 'sharing equitably benefits arising from the use of traditional knowledge', an activity given a novel, not to say Orwellian, turn by the recent habit among certain rapacious TNCs of patenting genetic resources. This capitalising tendency, even when it is not so grotesque as that, combined with the romantic externalisation and exaltation of nature, are the conditions within which, by and large, discourse about environmental sustainability takes place. They colour that well-known and, in some contexts, valuable debate about the shift from peasant husbandry to the capitalist domination of nature, though we are inclined to think that the main use of that debate lies in criticising techniques rather than principles. Raymond A. Rogers expressed the matter concisely in considering the principal current use of 'sustainability': '[It is used] as if nature is a factory producing an annual surplus available for human exploitation; as if it is possible to find the dotted line in nature that says exploit to here and stop.'[43]

Robert Chambers has spent much of his life insisting that progress can only lie in empowering the poor and he has set out the argument again in one of his more recent works.[44] In it he says that '[s]ustainability means that long-term perspectives should apply to all policies and actions, with sustainable livelihoods as objectives for present and future generations', an objective leading to what he calls 'responsible well-being'. First in his list of elements which might achieve this state includes 'combining and balancing the state and the market, to benefit, serve and empower the poor'.[45] This view lies very close to that of Martin W. Lewis and is subject to similar criticism. We may not doubt the heroism of such an endeavour, but we may reasonably be unconvinced about its chances of success because it disregards those intimate relationships between contemporary states and the market on which we have already remarked. We may offer one simple example in the field of whatever might count as environmental sustainability.

During much of the furore about genetically modified (GM) crops, particularly in the course of 1997, the agrichemical group Monsanto, together with other similar TNCs, engaged heavily in the debate about the safety of genetic modification. The argument raged about its effects on existing stocks and on wild plants, but the critics of the companies were on difficult ground since they were compelled to distinguish in some way between these new techniques promoted by the TNCs and the traditional techniques of cross-breeding and so on which have produced the world's present stock of food crops. Agrichemical TNCs, with an eye to the main financial chance, seem successfully to have modified plant genes in ways which will increase the dependency of farmers on the TNCs' other chemical products, but few of these corporations were bold enough to suggest that this would not have unquantifiable environmental consequences. Nonetheless, the TNCs largely succeeded in containing the argument within the realm of safety where they can almost certainly persuade enough people, particularly those in government or those whose research facilities depend on corporate sponsorship, that these risks are minimal and that the possibility of massively increased food production will far outweigh them. Early in 1999 the position changed quite dramatically with the verification of major work describing the malign effects of modified potatoes on rats. An earlier burial of a report by a group headed by distinguished scientist, Dr Arpad Pusztai, had resulted in the attempted destruction of that scientist's reputation, the closure of the research group and his dismissal, quite possibly under government pressure, from the scientific institute which had employed him.

Environmentalists certainly have reason to be worried, particularly since a group of twenty-one other eminent scientists have publicly supported Dr Pusztai's findings,[46] but they are fighting only half the battle. Scientists, particularly those employed by TNCs, tend to be enthusiasts for their products and it is worth bearing in mind that they gave us, for example and among many other benefits, Thalidomide and nuclear pollution. No one can doubt that there are risks, but the TNCs will bank on the way that history is littered with risky human enterprise and, in general, environmental arguments suggesting that genetically modified food crops are dangerous have, in the absence of much in the way of hard evidence, to depend on awful warnings about unquantifiable peril. This may change with the confirmation of Dr Pusztai's findings, though, at the time of writing, it is safe to predict that the TNCs will fight a major rearguard action, even though, early in 2000, Blair was compelled to make a U-turn in British government policy in the matter. Safety is an important question, but it is also part of a far larger issue which has, to a considerable degree, been left unexamined. It is the issue of the ownership and control of the greater part of the world's farming environment and of the bulk of the world's food chain.

This lacuna is particularly odd since we have the example of the notorious 'Green Revolution' in our recent past. In it cereals were genetically modified and new varieties, known originally as 'high yield varieties' and later as 'modern varieties' (MVs), were introduced. First developed in Mexico and the Philippines and subsequently planted widely throughout the Third World, MVs did result in substantially increased production despite a number of disease, pest and storage problems. There were other difficulties: the new seeds were dependent on extensive irrigation, particularly in areas where water was in short supply and often needed for the production of more socially useful crops; expensive chemicals were necessary for their protection. Crops produced from MVs were suited to the food commodity market and, as a consequence, were most successful on large plantations. Peasant small farmers could not afford the seeds or the chemicals, their commonly effective irrigation systems were undermined or simply seized, and many of them were ousted from their land to make way for TNC agribusiness.[47] Cheap cereals were produced, but not for or by the poor; these 'revolutionary' plants were best suited to the large, environmentally disastrous, mono-cultural plantations and simply became part of worldwide commodity agriculture.

Devotees of market capitalism have always defended their actions as beneficial to humanity in the long run, whatever unfortunate slips may take place on the way. Thus land seizures in the interests of modern farming designed to maximise profits have always been justified as 'improvements'.[48] Similarly, genetic modification has been dressed up as the key to food security, yet a closer look at what actually happens in the manufacturing process gives us something more like the truth. Once again the company is Monsanto (until recently it was, after all, the largest of the biotechnological businesses in the food industry) whose immensely successful weedkiller, Round Up (its active constituent is glyphosate), comes to the end of its patent in the year 2000. For some time the corporation has been developing genetically engineered strains of seeds which will produce crops able to resist glyphosate – it will sell these to farmers accompanied by a condition that the resultant crops be sprayed with Round Up, rather than any rival brand containing the chemical, which will kill surrounding weeds but leave the resistant crops intact.[49] Round Up is, of course, extremely efficient and is said not to damage the soil or water courses – but the deserts of, for example, East Anglia, are testimony to the effectiveness of such agents in destroying agricultural weeds and, therefore, the habitats that were essential to the older ecosystems. Poor farmers persuaded into the purchase of genetically modified seeds, particularly in countries where seed banks have been expropriated, will, of course, be further impoverished by having to pay for an additional expensive herbicide.

Genetic modification is intended, among other things, to deal with the problems of pests and diseases, but it goes hand in hand with genetic patenting. 'To critics [as the *Guardian* pointed out in a punchy leader] Monsanto is part of a profit-hungry industry protected by legal patents. Obsessed with commercial secrecy, monopolising research spending and now so close to liberal governments that it looks like a double act.'[50] Even in the wildly improbable event of genetically modified crops and animals settling down without causing radical and major change in, or damage to, the environment as it is conventionally understood, the economic and social consequences for huge numbers of the world's poor will be, as in the Green Revolution, catastrophic. If our argument for recognising human constructs as part of nature, of the environment, is accepted then any such catastrophe would render genetic modification and patenting ecologically unsustainable. We should in this context recall an actual instance of TNC attacks on farmers in the pressure brought by the World Bank and the IMF on the government of Zimbabwe to agree to the sale of the national seed bank to private corporations and thus denying farmers free access to their own resources.[51] What this example, together with many others, underlines is that the market-led scramble for all productive resources invariably, because of the nature of capital, results in the further impoverishment of the already poor.

Monsanto's actions also illustrate a major change in the ways that TNCs operate. In allowing genetically modified seeds to be subject to Intellectual Property Rights under the Marrakesh Agreement,[52] the WTO has enabled TNCs to move from direct ownership to the absolute control of the means of production. This can have results which would be comic if they were not so serious: Monsanto, in a curious little letter to the *Guardian* (26 September 1998), virtuously claimed not to have 'opted against' separating and, presumably, labelling genetically modified soya beans since they neither grew, shipped nor processed them. Separation and labelling must, their spokesperson remarked, be a matter for farmers, food-processors and, presumably, distributors. The letter goes on to claim that the corporation has done everything required of it to ensure the safety of its seeds but suggests that it might just have been at fault in not doing enough to 'inform consumers about GM foods'. 'Disingenuous' is the word which, not unreasonably, springs to our minds when considering this missive.

All the major corporations in the food industry are searching for ways in which to control the human food chain as completely as they can in order to make the greatest possible return for their shareholders, that, after all, is what corporations are for. GM seeds and plants are not only part of that endeavour, they are also part of a Promethean attempt at the control and reorganisation of nature for profit. Industrial farming is the form of agriculture most suited to the production of food for international consumption and this is as true for, say, sugar, cereals or soya beans as it is for the luxurious *mangetout* peas or the French beans grown in places as far apart as Guatemala and Kenya for the middle-class market. This explains why virtually all public accounts of MVs concentrated on how green they are and not on how revolutionary or, more correctly, how counter-revolutionary they are. Agriculture itself is increasingly seen by the governments of indebted countries as a resource to be exploited in the struggle for hard currency and, even though traditional peasant farming has constantly been shown to be substantially more productive than mono-cropping plantations,[53] peasants are increasingly being pushed off their land into wage labour or into landless destitution. TNCs have not yet entirely disengaged themselves from direct involvement in these humanly destructive processes, but they are increasingly doing so, leaving the less profitable dirty work to indigenous intermediaries and their states. We have written elsewhere about the contribution that all this has also made to recent humanitarian disasters and the part it plays in the agendas of humanitarian operations of relief;[54] our purpose here is to point to an important conditioning factor in any consideration of environmental or ecological sustainability in development.

It is here that the ideological conflict is most acute. On the one hand there is a battle between the assumptions made by those sympathetic development professionals in the INGOs and in some state agencies and the assumptions made by the dominant economic and political interests of their own states and of the TNCs operating from within them. On the other there is a simultaneous conflict between those who are, so to say, being 'developed' and who have changing needs and aspirations and the combination of development professionals and the dominant economic and political interests of the states from which they come. The ground over which the first of these two battles is being fought in environmental terms has been admirably described by Miguel A. Altieri. He writes of the inexorable shift within capitalist countries from the older and diversified kinds of farming to mono-cropping, its technological and chemical 'fixes', its ecological diseases and so on. In his conclusion he remarks that:

> Given the realities of capitalism, resource conserving practices are not profitable for farmers. The expectation that a set of policy changes could bring a renaissance of diversified or small scale farms may be unrealistic, because it negates the existence of economies of scale in agriculture and ignores the political power of agribusiness corporations and current trends set forth by globalisation.[55]

Altieri has US agribusiness principally in mind, but his reference to globalisation makes clear that the argument applies just as forcefully everywhere else. In the same issue of *Monthly Review*, R.C. Lewontin takes up the story in an account of the proletarianisation of farmers by 'the capitalist transformation of agriculture'. He describes the control, following the recent explosion in the categories of things which may be patented, by companies like Ciba-Geigy, Monsanto, DuPont and Dow, not only of farming inputs like genetically modified seed, but of farming methods and outputs. It is a system eminently suited to the rapid expansion of contract farming in the Third World,[56] but Lewontin remarks that there are other ways of keeping peasant farmers in line. He reminds us that a large part of our agricultural imports from the Third World 'consists in qualitatively unique materials like coffee, flavourings, essences, and food oils with special properties'. All these imports are produced by labour-intensive methods in poor countries which are often inherently unstable because of their poverty. Consequently they become 'prime targets for gene transfer into domestic species which will be grown as speciality crops under contract to processors'. He offers an example of the successful substitution, by a company called Calgene, of a genetically modified strain of rape seed for palm oil in the production of 'soaps, shampoos, cosmetics and food products' – a substitution which has had direct effects on workers in palm oil plantations in the Philippines.[57] We shall consider, in the chapters which follow, why TNCs need permanent innovation, state structures, state organisation of resources, infrastructure and planning and why they need to substitute technology for labour.

Here, we may return to Chambers' assertion that empowerment of the poor is central to sustainable development and to our dissection of the ways in which people from our societies, including development professionals and members of INGOs, confront the societies of the world's poor. But it is worth bearing a cautionary tale in mind. Development workers and analysts, sometimes including the present authors, have frequently commented on the way in which, for a variety of socio-economic reasons, peasants or landless people have either been forced into cultivating marginal land, or have been pushed economically into degrading their formerly adequate environment, and so have added, inadvertently, to ecological problems. While often it may be true that peasant farmers are frequently forced into environmentally destructive practices, care must be taken in determining when this is the case. We may quote the well-known, but nonetheless instructive, case recently revived by James Fairhead and Melissa Leach, who pointed out that ever since the French colonised what is now the Republic of Guinea, '[p]atches of dense, verdant, semi-deciduous rain forest [which] tower over expanses of grassy savanna' in the prefecture of Kissidougou have been seen as the surviving remnants of some great forest. It was thought that it had been destroyed by shifting cultivation which, right up until today, has continued to pose a threat to agriculture, tree cropping, water tables and climate. Fairhead and Leach have reminded us that this account is a product of an industrialised world view, these patches of dense forest were not remnants but 'islands [in the] savanna [which] owed their existence to inhabitants who had encouraged them to form around savanna settlements'.[58] As we have said, this is a cautionary tale and it would be rash to generalise from it; we offer it solely as a crude comment on the uncertainties involved in assessing environmental degradation and damage to ecosystems. It would not, we feel, be stretching matters too far to connect those mistaken interpretations of the Kissidougou landscape with the observers' culturally romantic desire to 'look on nature', in this case forests, with that 'sense sublime/Of something far more deeply interfused' allied to an automatic assumption that, for whatever reason, the peasant population had degraded their own environment. Above all, this story should raise questions about the measures used to establish sustainability.

In the next chapter we shall make the point that even if we allow economics the doubtful sobriquet of 'science', whether or not we add Carlyle's epithet 'dismal', we are describing a discipline inextricably entwined with the social, political and ideological assumptions of the society in which it is practised, that we have to see it as inseparable from both politics and philosophy. It, too, is pervaded by that same solipsistic, romantic idealism with which we approach environmental sustainability. Equally, the latter cannot, in any serious sense, be divorced from the economic imperatives of the society in which it is being advocated. Yet that divorce is constantly attempted by development professionals, particularly in the major INGOs. 'Sticking plaster' development is as well-known as 'sticking plaster' humanitarian assistance, indeed Bob Geldof clearly recognised the latter in naming his charity 'Band-Aid'. In it, local problems are identified, sometimes as a complex, programmes involving a variety of projects are mounted with varying degrees of participation from the people for whom they are designed; where they succeed they are offered to neighbouring communities as exemplars.[59] Recently this process has become more marked as the fashion for democratically organised micro-projects has increased, partly in response to the obvious and dramatic failures of many larger programmes.

Throughout the so-called developing world countless local agricultural, rural infrastructural, conservationist projects have been mounted, increasingly organised democratically and with an eye to their more or less successful continuation (sustainability). Expert advice, where it is needed, is often available and there is rarely a shortage of professionals who can produce intelligent analytical reports on the nature of the immediate difficulties. In general, however, much of it is like the treatment of cancer – will the patient survive beyond the first five years after the remedy has been attempted? Sustainability is frequently calculated in terms merely of the ability of a project to survive the funding period rather than in terms of its relationship to the macro-economic circumstances in which it finds itself. For example, Willem Kastelein in an interesting article in the *ILEIA Newsletter* (July 1988) discussed the development of irrigation in the Peruvian Andes. He was writing about the problems faced by smallholders farming in relatively high valleys (2,000 to 3,500 metres) which have semi-arid climates. Kastelein's article was about irrigation and although he mentioned one of the most important difficulties, the departure of able-bodied men for economic opportunities elsewhere or because of political violence, he did not discuss it. He did point to the consequent importance of incorporating women in 'formal irrigation organisations'; perhaps, in a longer article, he would have discussed the importance of incorporating them whether or not the men had left.

It is, of course, important that smallholders in the Andes should be helped in every way possible to irrigate their plots, but it is also important to consider what is happening to these communities. Agriculture in Peru accounts for about 10 per cent of GDP and employs around 35 per cent of the labour force. Many of the men leaving their Andean plots will be doing so either for industrial work, or for work in the mono-cropping plantations producing coffee, cotton or sugarcane or, just as probably, for work in the 121,000 hectares devoted to coca leaf. It is estimated that '85% of coca cultivation is for illicit production; most ... is shipped to Colombian drug dealers'.[60] The state is an oligarchy under the presidency of Alberto Fujimori who has repeatedly claimed, though with decreasing credibility, that the present is a period of 'transition', presumably to some form of democratic rule. Peru's total external debt is above US$23 billion and the country is under severe pressure from the IMF and the World Bank. Like so many other countries in this position, it is attempting to export its way out of trouble, principally, in order of importance, with copper, fishmeal, zinc, crude petroleum, lead, silver, coffee and cotton – its two largest markets are the EU and the USA. It is precisely in circumstances like these that smallholdings of the kind discussed by Kastelein become increasingly unviable and irrelevant to the state's economy. We do not suggest that this is to be commended, merely that it calls into question the sustainability of this particular environmental programme and others like it.

Tunisia provides a similar example, with slightly, but importantly, differing causes. It is a country of some nine million people with a *per capita* GNP of US$1,790. Its principal exports are crude petroleum, garments and manufactured fertilisers and its main markets are within the EU. Agriculture is also important, though not as valuable as other exports, and it employs about 24 per cent of the population. Tunisia's total external debt is in the region of US$9.5 billion and, judging by the 1998 reports from the World Bank (which thinks highly of the economy), will increase substantially as the country invests in 'modernisation'. Imports are running at 71 per cent of exports, debt servicing accounts for a little under 19 per cent – a healthy balance, but one in danger of being seriously eroded by the rapid increase in the costs of modernising infrastructure.[61]

A not insubstantial part of Tunisia's agricultural export earnings come from the cultivation of dates in the Saharan oases in the south of the country. Date palms rely on irrigation and, in the past, this meant that cultivation took place close to natural springs. More recently irrigation has been extended allowing date palms to grow on about 7,600 hectares surrounding sixty-eight oases – an extension which has made substantially increased demands on the water tables. Traditionally, farming families living in the oases ran a triple-layer cropping system consisting of date palms, fruit trees and a ground crop; this not only made efficient use of water, it actually conserved both water supplies and soil. To a very considerable degree this arrangement has been replaced by mono-cropping plantation methods with inadequate and wasteful irrigation systems. These date plantations and the new methods are often introduced by absentee entrepreneurs who increasingly represent contemporary patterns of ownership. Observers analysing the water problems pointed to the need not only to improve water efficiencies but, as a means of doing so, to re-establish the three-layer system of cropping.[62] What was missing from this otherwise admirable report by Mechergui and Vuren was any consideration of the socio-economic circumstances surrounding not only this kind of agriculture in Tunisia, but all kinds.

It is no accident that considerable areas around the oases subjected to this examination are owned by absentees. The World Bank has encouraged substantial 'modernisation' in the country's agriculture which has been accelerated by a recent free trade agreement with the EU. From January to July 1988, the Bank had lent Tunisia US$42 million to improve water resources much of which will be devoted to the production of food exports. A further US$50 million has been advanced for improvements to infrastructure which will also benefit the mono-cropping food exporters. Even more importantly US$98.7 million has been provided to support the transfer of businesses to the private entrepreneurial sector.[63] What Mechergui's and Vuren's report essentially calls for is a return to something like traditional farming and, indeed, the editors of the *ILEIA Newsletter* seem uneasily to have been aware of this. They added a text box which included the sentence 'The *Institut des Regions Arides* … in cooperation with the International Centre on Agricultural Research in Dryland Agriculture … are now trying to adapt these traditional systems to existing economic conditions.' First among those conditions is the stultifying effect of the high cost of money on investment in projects whose benefits only appear in the long term. States may borrow money more cheaply than private companies, the Tunisian government could subsidise the return to more sustainable practices, but free trade agreements of the kind it has entered into, to say nothing of the WTO, commonly forbid such interventions.

It would be foolish to question the importance of reports of the kind written by Mechergui and Vuren; what is at issue for us is the failure, not of this one report, but of the entire culture from which such reports spring. It is a culture that cannot afford to recognise that these reports and the consequent projects are, at best, piecemeal solutions to grave problems created by current market ideologies and, at worst, micro-projects as museum exhibits. That would mean abandoning some wider, if ill-defined, concept of agrarian, environmental sustainability for the measurement of sustainability in terms of enabling these people or those communities to survive until they are swept up into the dominant economy.

Those concerned with environmental sustainability in the industrialised world are fighting a valiant rearguard action, even though, as we observed earlier, they may be fighting on the wrong ground. What concerns us is the sense that development workers and some national development policies, often marked by that battle within the capitalist world, incorporate capital's romantic values in their desire to see the re-establishment of environmentally sound peasant farming.[64] To do this calls for project policies of local persuasion and encouragement, often thought of as local empowerment, as exemplary counterweights to the destructive advance of agribusiness. It is certainly true that some forms of empowerment do follow from these activities, but the problem is one of scale. Even large, environmentally sustainable projects touch only the edges of the immense Third World rural populations and have virtually no effect on the practices of globalised agribusiness. It is for this reason that much development activity is merely palliative; it is often first-aid carried out by stretcher-bearers brought in by the enemy to lend some kind of humanitarian gloss to their otherwise totally exploitative enterprises. That romanticism, that way of regarding nature both as property and as the source of and repository for our finer moments, renders us helpless in the face of the overriding financial and developmental priorities of the society which produced that vision. Harvey and Lovelock have, in their differing ways, made the point that we are unlikely to be able to destroy our planet, we only have the capacity to make it a good deal less pleasant. We may add that the greater part of that unpleasantness would be visited on the world's poor, thus it is that any argument for environmental or ecological sustainability has to be made understanding the philosophical, economic, political and teleological context in which it is being offered.

Much of the argument surrounding environmentally sustainable development is simply confused, largely because the parties to it rarely distinguish the phenomena they are discussing. Environmental sustainability in development comes, as a concept, not only with the ideological baggage we have been discussing, but actually conjures up different things for the various parties engaged in it. Climate change offers an excellent example. Few people doubt the evidence offered by scientists that the globe is warming, that the ozone layer and the ionosphere are thinning dangerously, that seas are rising and that sudden and catastrophic climate change is possible. Doubters may become even fewer as disasters like the recent and appalling destruction in Central America, India and Mozambique become more frequent. Nor do many doubt that whatever natural climatic cycles may be involved, the process has been accelerated, possibly exaggerated, by the human production and discharge into the atmosphere of damaging gases and particles. Even those who, for whatever reason, remain sceptical at least recognise the political necessity of taking climate change seriously. Running through the furore surrounding the issue has been the repeated claim that industrial and transport development depending on the unregulated burning of fossil fuels is unsustainable. This, too, has not been denied and the problem is widely recognised – to the point where we occasionally hear suggestions that necessary industrial development in poorer countries should not follow the destructive path taken by industrial nations.

Admirable rhetoric is rarely lacking, but it is scarcely surprising that politics and capital are unengagingly mimetic, one of the other. Both operate in closed, short-termist cycles. Politicians are trapped in what they see as the need to satisfy a curiously blind electorate and will do nothing, for fear of the next election, which might alienate their main support. Capital, business, is trapped in the need to deliver returns on investment calculable over even shorter periods than those allowed to politicians. Since both parties are in power, they batten on each other in searching for the easiest way of dealing with what might be troublesome long-term commitments. Nowhere has this dismal tale been illustrated so vividly as in governmental responses to the looming problems of climatic change. In the preamble to the UNFCCC agreed at Rio, the 'parties' noted 'that change in the Earth's climate and its adverse effects are a common concern of humankind'. They registered their 'concern' about the emissions of greenhouse gases and 'noted' that, historically, most of them came from the industrialised world but 'that the share of global emissions originating in developing countries will grow to meet their social and development needs'.

Politicians from the industrialised states, urged on by their energy and transport lobbies, ensured that nothing too dangerous to their interests should be built into any agreement. In the event two fatally weak paragraphs were agreed (Article 4, section 2 (a) and (b)). The first is an agreement that the developed nations would take measures to reduce emissions; the second committed them to tell the world, within six months following the entry into force of the Convention, about their policies for reductions aimed at returning to 1990 levels. Neither paragraph was sufficiently specific to be more than a recommendation. In the years following Rio some effort to reduce emissions was made, but these were offset by increased activity; in 1997, shortly before the Kyoto summit, US emissions were said to have increased by 3.4 per cent over the previous year.[65] A few days after that report was released, President Clinton, succumbing to pressure from the oil and automobile lobbies, announced that the USA would postpone its target date for beginning to revert to 1990 emission levels to the year 2017.[66] He justified this twenty-year delay by referring to the long-term nature of the problem – we may also observe that it moved the issue several years beyond the end of his presidency.

Kyoto, of course, produced that bizarre agreement in which permissible emissions of greenhouse gases would be based on the sizes of national populations, but those states not producing the amounts they were permitted could be allowed to sell their excess capacity to others who were exceeding their targets. Within states individual industrial facilities or industries like transport, would be licensed to emit gases up to a certain level and those able to reduce their emissions to below that level would be permitted to sell their unused rights to other plants or industries. Inevitably this has led to calls by international industrial bodies for legislation allowing for the trading of permits in the stock exchanges. The International Petroleum Exchange seems to have led the way.[67] So it is that what was conceived by the world at large to be an attempt at cleaning up an industrial act has become a new investment project for those compulsive gamblers who inhabit the world's bourses. Campaigners for the reduction of greenhouse gases see the present position as unsustainable because they fear, with considerable justification, some catastrophic change in climate. Industrialists and, by and large, politicians calculate matters differently. For them a serious onslaught on emissions would be a threat to their environment of competition, profitability and, because it could dramatically affect the lives of the voting middle classes, re-election. Drastic action to circumvent something which has not quite happened and which could gravely damage this other account of an environment is, in their terms, unsustainable.

Environmental sustainability is about nature, but nature includes humanity. Harvey has made a comprehensive case for taking that interaction of nature and humanity into account and, because it leads us to an understanding of the social and, indeed, the capitalist, production of nature, it becomes difficult to deal with environmental issues on their own. In 1997, the Nineteenth Special Session of the United Nations General Assembly, better known, when it is remembered at all, as 'Earth Summit II' took place in New York to examine progress on the issues of sustainable development raised in Rio. The United Nations Environment and Development – UK Committee has published a surprisingly optimistic account of the proceedings in which it reports the Summit's review of that progress and although it concluded that there is now wide international support for the idea of sustainable development, there is little evidence of action.[68]

We may summarise our position by remarking on the obvious: environmental sustainability is not a univocal concept, it can only be interpreted in the context of the presuppositions of the utterer. Its obverse is marginally easier to use: few would doubt, for example, that irresponsible farming methods employed in reducing the greater part of the rich ecosystems of East Anglia to a virtual desert, kept productive only by chemical engineering, are environmentally unsustainable. In that case, as in many others, the argument becomes one about whether, in a wider context, the benefits to humanity were greater than the loss. Similarly, it would be difficult to deny that chemical onslaughts on the ozone layer are unsustainable because holes in it permit extensive damage to the world's food chains and allow substantial increases in the penetration of our atmosphere by carcinogenic rays from the sun. In both instances the response was to search for ways allowing the modes of production, which were the ultimate causes of the damage, to continue by tinkering with the immediate causes – the destruction of ecosystems, the use of alternative chemicals – in the interests of maintaining 'sustainable' levels of profit. It is in the light of this perception that we must then consider the calls for sustainable development, whether in agriculture or in industry, in the Third World. Before we may pose the question 'Is x sustainable?' we must first discover who is asking.

4
Opportunities Legally Monopolised[1]

In the penultimate paragraph of our introduction, we remarked, unflatteringly, on the confessional nature of economics – a view expressed slightly differently in a quip attributed to George Bernard Shaw: 'If all economists were laid end to end, they would not reach a conclusion.' Quite apart from radically differing and often irreconcilable approaches in economics there is a further semantic difficulty: economists have, for generations, been dogged by the assumption that their subject is a 'science' (in many universities it is actually called 'economic science'). Although the habit lingers, numbers of contemporary economists either reject the label as a hindrance or simply ignore it, but non-economists, working in the worlds of finance and politics, continue to think of the discipline as some sort of applied science operating with laws at least as reliable as those of gravity.[2] We feel that they would be better served if they understood that economics is independent and not in need of such categorisation, but, if insecurity compels them, then they might do better to recognise it as some part of philosophy, sociology or, even, politics.

Economists themselves are now less inclined to be constrained by labels and recognise the variety of choices involved in their analyses:

> The only reason for studying economics is to understand economic argument ... *Every* economic issue can be approached and understood from different points of view. Economic issues are *always* controversial. Alternative analyses conceptualise economic

problems differently, and consequently theorise the sequence of events differently.[3]

This point has also been made by Eric Hobsbawm in casting an historian's eye on both earlier and contemporary economic theory:

> Unless I am greatly mistaken, economic theory facilitates the choice between decisions, and perhaps develops techniques for making, implementing and monitoring decisions, but does not itself generate positive policy-making decisions.[4]

But there is some way to go before we can dislodge the generality of financiers and the ministers of their governments from their tendency to justify catastrophic political and financial choices as economically imperative. In a famous passage ending in almost existential despair, Keynes first suggested that trade between nations need not be ruthlessly competitive, that nations might 'learn to provide themselves with full employment' and that international trade could become 'a willing and unimpeded exchange of goods and services in conditions of mutual advantage'. He ended by casting against this somewhat over-refulgent hope the idiocy of 'practical men':

> The ideas of economists and political philosophers, both when they are right and when they are wrong, are more powerful than is commonly understood. Indeed the world is ruled by little else. Practical men, who believe themselves to be quite exempt from any intellectual influences, are usually the slaves of some defunct economist. Madmen in authority, who hear voices in the air, are distilling their frenzy from some academic scribbler of a few years back.[5]

We have laboured this point and will, indeed, expand it throughout this chapter simply because it obviously has considerable implications for any meaning we wish to attach to that neoteric phrase, 'economic sustainability'.

Economic activity is an area in which 'practical men' of power have typically attached a sort of hegemonic rationality to their theories. Sanity, security, progress, almost all desirable things, these 'practical men' insist, can be ours only if we allow the market to be free – other economic courses will spell ruin. This bizarre view continues to be held despite compelling evidence to the contrary. 'IMF Cuts Growth Forecasts – Outlook Is Bleakest for Seven Years', 'Global Fortunes Teeter on Pyramid Schemes of Sand', 'Markets Peer into Abyss over Brazil'[6] were headlines representative of all the serious English broadsheets during the financial crisis in the autumn of 1998, yet, as the world seemed to be tumbling about them, these 'practical men' – free marketeers – insisted on their mantras. We do not, of course, have to look far for the reason since these headlines referred to the markets in currencies, in stocks and shares and phenomena like the relatively new form of reckless gambling known as 'hedge funds'.[7] In all of them, capital becomes both producer and product – a concept to which we must return – fortunes are made, and sometimes lost, in what, by its nature, is a hermetic world. The counters used by these compulsive gamblers, also known as 'bankers' or 'market traders' or some other such euphemism, in their obsessive pursuit of financial return, are the livelihoods of countless relatively and absolutely poor people. Evidently 'practical men' have substantial vested interests in maintaining their control of economic theory, though the implosion of free-marketeering in South East Asia in 1997 and the consequent Gadarene rush to protectionism[8] by those who, immediately before the event, proclaimed the immutability of the economic laws of *laissez-faire*, may possibly inspire them towards more modest ambition. It is important to remember that although financial markets have recovered, the industrial economies of South East Asia have been severely damaged.

We ended the last chapter by pointing out that the decision whether or not '*x*' is environmentally sustainable depended on the presuppositions of the judge. This is, of course, no less true in determining economic sustainability. Environmentalists and economists are both known cheerfully to insist that the sustainability of the other's practice is dependent on submission to their criteria. At this stage in global economic uncertainty, we are quite at liberty to assert that neo-liberal, free-market economic practice is unsustainable in its own terms. But this is unhelpful since responses to crisis from capital have not led to the abandonment of the concept, but to its limitation, to its adjustment, to the point only where some recovery is thought to be possible; and recovery, in capital markets, is frequently measured in the shortest of possible terms. Economic sustainability in financial markets is understood, by the practitioners, in the arcane terms of the market itself. Social consequences, including the loss of livelihoods and homes, are by-products of the process and, in general, are only interesting as they relate to its successful continuation. It is common for the institutions of capital to act in ways which will increase unemployment and poverty if those ways are judged to be necessary to the survival of markets, their banking systems and an increase in their rate of profit.[9] In this they are supported by their client right-wing social-democratic governments and we may take Tony Blair's speech at the 1998 Lord Mayor's Banquet as an example. He supported his belief that long-term growth is only possible in a tightly controlled monetarist economy and that he would resist short-termist responses to approaching recession even at the cost of increased unemployment.[10] Any conclusion that free-market economic practice is unsustainable depends on the very unfree-trade principle that the lives of ordinary people must be a factor in any economic decision. This excursion into the obvious is made as further illustration of the pitfalls lurking in the syntax of sustainability.

Few would take the trouble to quarrel with Einstein's crude definition of the environment quoted in the last chapter: 'the environment is everything that isn't me'. In economics no such simplicity is really possible since any economic analysis, or principle, depends on prior decisions about starting points, or, more accurately, about the *political* or *philosophical* assumptions the enquirer wishes to substantiate. This becomes clear once it is recognised that economics is to do with the analysis of all aspects of valuation and that 'Adam Smith in the eighteenth century ... raised value as revealed in the market place to a dominant position.'[11] In their book *Why Economists Disagree*, Cole, Cameron and Edwards make a substantial argument for identifying three principal analytical economic theories. They see two main heirs to Smith – Thomas Robert Malthus and David Ricardo. Malthus, followed and expanded by, among others, Vilfredo Pareto and Milton Friedman, leads us to an economic theory of value which Cole *et al.* label 'subjective preference'. Ricardo, they suggest, gave rise to two other distinctive theories: one, by way of Thorstein Veblen, J.M. Keynes and J.K. Galbraith, they describe as the 'cost-of-production theory of value'; the other, via Karl Marx and Frederick Engels, Nikolai Bukharin,

Ernest Mandel and Charles Bettelheim, they call the 'abstract labour theory of value'. We have set out the broad continua in figure 4.1.[12]

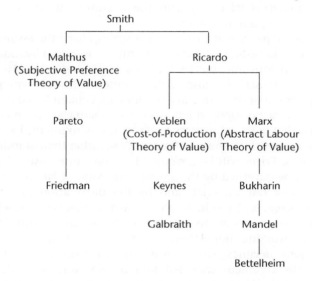

Figure 4.1 Economic progressions

We do not, for our purposes, need to follow Cole and his fellows through their arguments for identifying continua and categorising economic theories thus, but we must make use of their summaries which we shall contract yet further. The *subjective preference theory of value* is profoundly individualistic and begins by assuming that each individual will act so as to do her or his utmost to improve 'personal welfare or utility'. Consumption will be determined by this objective and by each individual's personal abilities in, and opportunities for, productive activity. Individuals are, nonetheless, economically inter-dependent and must exchange what they produce in the market-place. Exchange compels specialisation in forms of produc-tion: hence labour is socially divided. Prices will be fixed to reflect the cost of labour, the cost of entrepreneurship and its necessary profits, and interest for the investor. They will also depend on the willingness of the purchaser to buy. No contract to buy or sell is entered into in such a model, unless it is in the interests of the individual to do so. By this means of exchange 'personal welfare or utility' is rendered consonant with that of everyone else and the role of government is solely to ensure the 'maximum freedom for individual consumption decisions'.

The *cost-of-production theory of value* springs from the assumption, proposed by Ricardo, that value in the market is set not by individual decisions to consume, but by the choices of production. He advocated this approach because of the manifest injustices wrought by the application of those free-market principles championed by Adam Smith. It is a position which starts by looking at the materially possible, that is to say matters to do with environment, its control and the nature of the means of production, rather than at individual preferences. Prices will be governed by production costs which, in turn, will be governed by the amount and kind of labour, the sorts and costs of raw materials and by the distribution of proceeds between wages and profit. Ricardo added to this two further positions: if goods necessary to subsistence increase in quantity, then so does the working population; on the other hand, agricultural productivity declines with increases in the amount of cultivated land.[13] His argument then led him to the conclusion that free markets, of the kind advocated by the adherents of the subjective preference theory, lead inevitably to economic stagnation, an impoverished workforce and conspicuous consumption by the owners. This is because although, in theory, it is in the interests both of owners and of workers to produce as much as possible so as to maximise rewards, the division of reward will depend on the relative powers of the two parties. The owners will always try to reduce the costs of production and, in particular, the cost of labour, either by wage cutting or by the introduction of new technology. It is notorious that this results, on the one hand, in workers' opposition to technical change and, on the other, in the introduction of technical change solely in the interests of maximising profit. The consequent creation of mass unemployment is a threat to society. Solutions, for cost-of-production theorists, lie in pluralist politics and some sort of compromise between the conflicting parties refereed by government and bureaucracy – Anthony Giddens is one of the better known of its recent advocates.[14]

Cole has recently commented further on the work in which he and his fellows set out their categories:

In the mid-1980s I began to apply my mind to explaining why different 'scientific' theoretical perspectives appealed to different people as more or less plausible, leading to the publication of *Understanding Economics*. The argument went beyond *Why Economists Disagree* by seeing the different theories of value as reflections of different aspects of social exchange. All societies are characterized by a technical division of labour. People's productive activity is specialized: people do not consume what they produce. Hence there has to be exchange between producers and consumers. One theory of value sees the consumer as the economic dynamic, with the rate of exchange and therefore price reflecting the preferences of consumers – the subjective preference theory of value; alternatively the producer can be understood as the economic dynamic – the cost-of-production theory of value; or people can be seen as both producers and consumers, the citizen is the economic dynamic – the abstract labour theory of value. Theory was now related to experience rather than to ideas. And because consumers and producers are party to every economic transaction, such activity can always be differentially analysed in terms of alternative theories of value.[15]

The *abstract labour theory of value* is the name given, by Cole, Cameron and Edwards, to Marx's transformation of a Ricardian labour theory of value by the addition of two further concepts. Marx formulated the basis of his theory in the opening pages of *Capital* in his accounts of 'use-value' and 'exchange-value' and, above all, in his creation of the theory of 'surplus-value'. 'The usefulness of a thing makes it a use-value' and he supplemented this remark with a foot-noted quotation from John Locke: 'The natural worth of anything consists in its fitness to supply the necessities, or serve the conveniences of human life.' The use-value 'of a commodity is independent of the amount of labour required to appropriate its useful qualities'.[16] For use-value to be realised the object at issue must be used or consumed. Exchange-value, on the other hand, Marx first expresses as the quantification of the exchange of differing use-values, as in a system of barter: 'a quarter of wheat, for example, is exchanged for x boot-polish, y silk or z gold, etc.' Each of these things, in their respective quantities, has the same exchange-value as the wheat and each, like the wheat, has numerous exchange-values.

That respective quantity is, of course, all-important, a quarter of wheat is likely to have a smaller exchange-value in a society where wheat, or an equivalent, is relatively more plentiful than a quarter of gold. Marx uses this point to explain the crucial difference between the two sets of value: 'As use-values, commodities differ above all in quality while as exchange-values they can only differ in quantity, and therefore do not contain an atom of use-value.'[17] Exchange-values will, of course, vary both in place and in time but they all share the characteristic of being, in some sense, determined by the amount of labour involved in the production of the commodities to be exchanged. Marx describes exchange-values as being 'merely definite quantities of *congealed labour-time*'.[18] In this we find his concept of *abstract social labour* on which he built his entire theory of value. Ernest Mandel remarked that:

> The distinction between concrete labour, which determines the use-value of commodities, and abstract labour, which determines their value, is a revolutionary step forward beyond Ricardo of which Marx was very proud; indeed he considered it his main achievement, together with the discovery of the *general* category of surplus-value, encompassing profit, rent and interest.[19]

Useful labour is labour devoted to the making of things with use-value and may also be considered in two ways. The first is the value of the labour employed in the production of the useful object, a value which will be determined primarily (in our simple model) by the exchange-value of the object produced. Marx offers the example of a coat and ten yards of linen in which the value of the former is twice that of the latter; he extrapolates from this the second way of thinking about labour with the proposition that there are 'heterogeneous use-values ... [reflecting] ... heterogeneous forms of useful labour, which differ in order, genus, species and variety: in short, a social division of labour'.[20] While this differentiation may vary specifically in differing periods and places, in any 'particular society it is given'. Ironically misquoting Hegel,[21] he points out that, like the comparison between the exchange-values of gold and wheat, 'a smaller quantity of complex labour is considered equal to a larger quantity of simple labour.'[22] Commodities, in exchange-values, become mere 'quantities of congealed labour-time', but labour itself, no matter how differentiated in its production of use-value, counts 'only as being an expenditure of human labour-power'.[23] In other words, labour itself is commodified by the capitalist, becomes itself an exchange-value and may be sold and bought.

By dividing economic theory into three principal groups in this way, Cole and his fellows have fully exposed the degree to which analytical results are dependent not on the examination of undifferentiated phenomena presented, for one reason or another, to the economist, but on a strictly *political* selection, by the economist, of analytical tools. Nothing within economics can compel a choice of economic approach; it can only be made on the basis of prior decisions about the desired outcomes and must be justified on other grounds. An illustration of this may be found in Adam Smith's account of wages and profit[24] in which he asserts, on moral as well as practical grounds, that workers must be compensated for enforced idleness, danger in their occupations, the unpleasantness of their task and so on. He also rails against the oppressiveness of laws in eighteenth-century England which prevented the free movement of labourers and does so on the ground that it is intolerable for supposedly free people effectively to be imprisoned at the whim of local functionaries.[25] Images of sauces for geese and ganders spring to mind – just as we make this point about those systems we choose to criticise, so is it true of our own position. Which of the three approaches we favour must, by now, be obvious and we shall expect to justify our decision partly in the criticisms we offer in this chapter, but also in our discussion of sustainability and social justice in the next.

Our account of the concept of value central to Marx's economic thought (we discuss its third term – 'surplus-value' – below), truncated and vastly over-simplified though it is, nonetheless is adequate for our enquiry into the pre-suppositions commonly contained in the portmanteau idea of economic sustainability.[26] Eric Hobsbawm has recently reminded us of Kondratiev's 'long waves',[27] periods of expansion and contraction in economic activity each lasting for about fifty years, three of which were observed between 1792 and 1940. Hobsbawm maintains that despite the lack of any serious analysis of the idea or of the phenomena adduced by Kondratiev in its support and despite, also, the dismissal of the idea by many economists, it has served historians well as an instrument of prediction.

Accurate forecasts, allowing for small distortions caused by wars, might possibly warrant further exploration of Kondratiev's thesis, because if periods of economic decline are regular then concern about the imminent collapse of all, or large parts of, the system when they happen may be misplaced. We suspect that the question is probably less important than understanding what causes economic downturns. The decline in 1997–98 was so acute that it might better be described as free fall, no-one knew how it might be arrested and predictions of its universality were rife – this was also the common fear at the time of the Wall Street Crash of 1929. Whether, or not, the periodic massive international declines in stock markets will eventually spill over into some collapse of the system will depend less on factors within the strict workings of the market and more on social and political responses to it.

'Cycles', Kondratievian or otherwise, because they imply regularity and underlying stability, somehow dignify the progress of capital in a way that describing the patterns as a series of drunken lurches would not. Institutions of capital, by their nature, are competitive and are bound always to grow by increasing their returns. In the manufacturing and service sectors of capital this may be achieved by expanding markets, that is by finding new purchasers (for example, tobacco barons of the developed world pushing their addictive drugs to the poor in developing countries[28] and to children everywhere), by driving other companies out of existing markets (as in the case of supermarket and chain-store wars on smaller retailers) and by producing more in order to reduce prices and so to reach less affluent socio-economic groups. Increased production at lower prices may also be used, particularly by component manufacturers, to persuade companies making the finished product to become customers. Buried in that relationship is the notorious business of transfer pricing, a legal technique beloved of TNCs which is actually a disreputable mix of money-laundering, profit-taking and tax evasion. Several industries also rely on expanding the production of new items to provide larger returns which will also cover outstanding debts incurred in earlier stages of expansion – one famous example may be seen in mass-market paperback book publishing. None of this is an exact science and no matter how carefully markets are 'researched', simple opportunism dictates many of the choices. Finance capital, on the other hand, shadows the manufacturing sector by investing in success, whether actual or forecast. It lends the money that business needs in order to trade and expects to make a handsome profit either from the rate of interest agreed in the loan, or it sells the money and expects substantial dividends on the shares it has accepted in payment. It has a number of extremely profitable side-lines to that particular set of transactions, including the multiform gambling in stocks, shares and the hedge funds that we have already mentioned. Above all, at least in terms of risk, is gambling on the comparative values of currencies. As we remarked in Chapter 2, 'investors, like sheep, follow one another' and, in the case of currency speculation, since they are gambling on values placed on currencies by their fellows, what is actually happening in the states or regions concerned is of subsidiary importance. That curious case of mutual lunacy, led by George Soros and Norman Lamont, in which Britain was forced out of the European Exchange Rate Mechanism (ERM), was a fine example.

Problems are caused in particular by industry's constant over-production. For example, in the late 1990s the world found itself over-supplied with, among other things, motor vehicles and microchips. The manufacture of each had burgeoned in low-wage economies as TNCs fought to corner markets by producing in larger and larger quantities at lower and lower prices. Excessive rates of production were buttressed by astonishing levels of corruption – Indonesia, Malaysia, South Korea and the notorious 'sweetheart' deals set up by, among others, the British arms trade are all well-known examples. Rates of production in the period immediately before the 1997–98 collapse also helped to create an illusory sense of permanence which, in turn, stimulated astonishing levels of investment, particularly by Japanese financiers, in speculative building.

Governments also borrow, though generally more cheaply than companies, but the ways in which they do so can also affect global markets. Russia had, as Edward Luttwak pointed out, been badly affected by the global collapse of commodity prices, particularly oil, which seriously eroded its otherwise healthy trade balance.[29] Its government had been in the habit of short-term borrowing because by doing so they could keep immediate interest payments lower; Luttwak remarked that by April 1998 '40 billion dollars in rouble denominated Treasury bills were due for turn-over through the end of 1998'. Certificates of security, short-term bills, were themselves traded by the lenders, one of the other profitable side-lines available to finance capital. It was a system which worked well for several years until the South East and East Asian stock markets collapsed, a collapse reinforced by the vagaries of currency speculation – the gamblers sold everything they could for fear that the contagion would spread. According to Luttwak none of them took differences in circumstance into account and, by selling or redeeming their Russian short-term bills for what they could get at a time when falling commodity prices drastically reduced Russia's foreign currency earnings, virtually bankrupted the hitherto moderately healthy rouble economy.

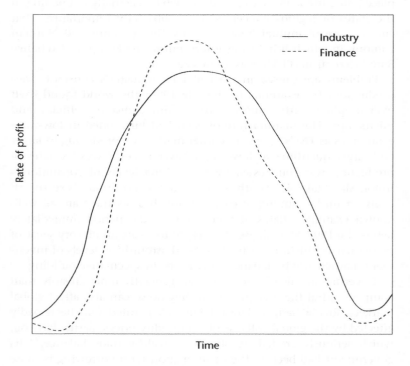

Figure 4.2   A typical relationship between financial and industrial capital

What emerges from this is the need to look more closely at cycles of expansion and decline. In practice there are two lines to be made on any graph plotting them. One is the curve described by what may loosely be called industry and the other is that described by finance capital, the administration of which is also an industry (figure 4.2). The dotted line represents the movement of finance capital through the banks, the multiplicity of stock markets and so on. Hobsbawm long ago pointed out that big money, either in banking or in private and corporate wealth, is generally unwilling to run the risk of engaging directly in industry, preferring instead to diversify its investment in the purchase of wide ranges of shares.[30] These may be shed in the international bourses at any moment at which their owners suspect that the companies in which they have shares may, for whatever reason, be at some risk of losing profitability, no matter how minutely. In our model, as industry begins to decline, finance, which enthusiastically over-extends itself when industry is booming, withdraws at a rate even faster than industrial decline, when it occurs, would seem to demand. This, in turn, adds to industry's difficulties and accelerates its decline yet further. It is important to remember that these gamblers do not shadow industry closely, but make their investments in the light of their own arcane rules.

If any of the cyclical theories of capital are accepted, then decline need not be terminal, that is, need not decline into massive slump. There will, of course, be casualties, chief and least considered among them all is the workforce and its dependants. Industrial history is littered with stories of the hardship and misery of the working class in times of depression. Some companies will be bankrupted, some will be absorbed into larger competitors, some money will be lost, but those corporations which survive the internecine competition for what remains of the market in its decline will emerge, when conditions change, in a strong position to launch the new expansionary phase. Of course, it is perfectly common for cycles of this kind to occur within sectors of the economy as well as in the economy as a whole.[31] Marx was familiar with yet another distinction, that these cycles may occur within a particular industry situated in different places and often separately owned – he pointed to the periodic rises in Indian cotton production between 1835 and 1865 which coincided with corresponding declines in US production.[32] A third variation may be the decline of one sector within an economy, balanced by the rise of another. For example, industrial agriculture may go into steep decline, as in parts of Northern Europe, while, say, the construction industry grows rapidly. Similarly, we are familiar with the contraction of much heavy industry within the OECD while it does quite well in several low-wage economies elsewhere. The huge change is the globalisation of finance and the corresponding patterns of share ownership and investment.

Much the same thing happened, though on a smaller scale, following the famous Wall Street Crash on 29 October 1929 which, in turn, led to widespread industrial collapse. Just as, during 1997–98 the principal Asian stock markets failed, one after the other, to be followed by those in Latin America and Russia, so, from 1929 to around 1933, calamity in the form of the Great Depression spread throughout much of the world. Although recovery in Europe and the United States began, a little uncertainly, in 1934, the effects of the Depression really only finally disappeared in the arming for, and the commencement of, World War II. Industrial capital relishes war because the price of weaponry is cost plus agreed profit, thus guaranteeing liquidity. This liquidity is enhanced because of the nature of the war commodities – you cannot drop a bomb twice. Why recovery should have depended on the outbreak of war and exactly how it happened are not our immediate concern, except to observe that the successful economies of the period from 1940 to 1960 were those whose governments adopted highly interventionist and unfree-market policies.[33] The substantial difference between the crash of 1929 and the present lies in the far greater globalisation of capital and the consequently greater reach of the effects of major decline.

Optimists might argue that the period 1940–97 is near enough to fifty years, particularly allowing for wars, to be seen as another of Kondratiev's cycles. In that case we may look forward to some recovery not too long after the end, when it comes, of the decline. An optimistic account presupposes a proportional regularity in which finance does shadow industry, no matter how cautiously, but, following periods of decline and retrenchment, both emerge to expand to newer and greater things; it is a process without obvious end. We might add that it is also a model without obvious logic nor with much in the way of historical support. In effect, it is an article of faith, like so much else in the armoury of free marketeers. The importance of this discussion lies less in the correctness, or otherwise, of the market propaganda offered by proponents of unregulated trade and investment and more in the extent to which the argument is divorced from the well-being of much of society. Margaret Thatcher understood this very well, hence her infamous remark: 'There is no such thing as Society. There are individual men and women, and there are families.'[34] Our optimists are committed to the alienation involved in the elevation of market values as the sole measure of economic and, therefore, social probity.

Throughout this chapter we have used the terms 'global' or 'globalisation' without stopping to define them and we should make clear what we mean. Marx and Engels could not have guessed at the forms to be taken by contemporary capitalism, but they certainly expected something in the nature of globalisation:

> The bourgeoisie has through its exploitation of the world-market given a cosmopolitan character to production and consumption in every country ... it has drawn from under the feet of industry the national ground on which it stood. All old-established national industries have been destroyed or are daily being destroyed. They are dislodged by new industries ... that no longer work up indigenous raw material, but raw material drawn from the remotest zones ... In place of the old local and national seclusion and self-sufficiency, we have intercourse in every direction, universal inter-dependence of nations ...
>
> The bourgeoisie ... compels all nations, on pain of extinction, to adopt the bourgeois mode of production; it compels them to introduce what it calls civilisation into their midst, *i.e.*, to become bourgeois themselves. In one word, it creates a world after its own image.[35]

This was not simple prescience, they knew that the process was in the nature of capitalism. It will quite possibly develop yet further and, at some point in the future, analyses will have to be refined further but, for the time being, change will be relatively slow, not the least because of the recent massive failures in market nerve. Helots of free-market ideology make globalism formulaic, everything may be globalised and they speak gravely, if inanely, of the 'global village'. Corporations, financial as well as industrial, act more cautiously, for them globalisation does not mean corporate mobility, nor does it normally mean the movement of their central activities to countries thought to be more financially attractive or less well-regulated than the states in which they were created. We have already mentioned the ways in which TNCs may shift parts of their operations, but their capital centre rarely moves very far from the apparent security of the OECD economies, particularly that of the USA.

Leo Panitch suggests that globalisation consists in:

i. an increase in markets following the collapse of the Soviet Union and the decisions by China and Vietnam to adopt capitalist economies;
ii. the hegemony of neo-liberal capitalist ideology and culture;
iii. the gradual and, as yet, incomplete emergence of a transnational ruling class (owners and directors of international corporations);
iv. a new and complex stage in worldwide capital accumulation;
v. the adaptation of nation states to the needs of worldwide capital accumulation.

Apropos of Panitch's first term, the World Bank, in its 1998/99 report, points out that in 1997 China received 31 per cent of the year's total foreign direct investment (FDI) in developing countries.[36] His account of the fourth element is the most important and we quote it in full:

[globalisation refers to] the new stage of capital accumulation on a world-scale, developing out of the contradictions of the post-war Keynesian/Bretton Woods order, which is characterised by a vast increase in the size, flow and speed of foreign direct investment and trade, and accompanied by an even more vast creation of international credit, currency flows, speculation, futures markets, and private and public debt.[37]

Not only is this the core of globalisation, but it is here, too, that capital most obviously becomes both producer and product, divorced from the classical forms of production and inhabiting a surreal trading world. Capital's 'products' have use- and exchange-values for an ever-decreasing number of consumers, rendering it cumulatively more unstable.

Within exchange-value is contained another concept introduced into economics by Marx, that of 'surplus-value'. At its simplest it is the difference in value between the time it takes a worker to cover her or his wages and costs and the time that he or she actually works.[38] Exchange-values are set not by a simple computation of the varieties of 'congealed labour-time' plus external costs, but by including the time for which the labourer is not paid. It is relatively easy to follow this basic process through the complexities of modern industry and commerce. For us, the point lies in the desire by the owners of capital to maximise surplus-value which they achieve by two means: reducing the workforce by automation and by the direct depression of wages. The latter may take the form either of wage-cuts, casualisation and so on, or of moving production to low-wage economies – one of the most notorious examples of relocating industry to reduce wage costs is found in the Mexican *maqiladoras*. Depressing wages, however, brings its own problems for capital which first became acute in Britain in the late eighteenth and early nineteenth centuries. Industrial capital had been developed by concentrating on the export market, but the labour for it was drawn from a large urban population rapidly increasing naturally and added to by further larger influxes from rural areas and, by the mid-nineteenth century, mass immigration from Ireland. Poverty in the working class was such that few of its members could afford more than the barest essentials of life and were not, despite being a large proportion of the British population, capable of providing a home market for most of the goods they were producing. Industry and finance became, as a consequence, even more dependent on overseas markets for realising their surplus-value.[39]

A century or more later many things have changed. Socio-political, economic and demographic changes have produced a larger and more affluent middle class. Capital's need for labour in its post-World War II expansionary period allowed for the emergence of effective trades unions and wage bargaining and so, to a substantial degree, enriched workers sufficiently for them to become, from capital's point of view, important domestic markets. Since the mid-1970s, monetarist capital has done its utmost to roll back that progress or to reduce worker power by the kinds of agreement touched on in Chapter 2. These agreements sought to limit wage increases and rights to strike, sometimes in return for small share offers which usually entailed a further surrender to management of control over working conditions and processes.[40] But despite capital's failure completely to impoverish its domestic work-forces, for huge areas of capital operation a domestic market, no matter how strong, can be no more than a cushion for those moments when export markets, for whatever reason, weaken. Competing industries of all kinds can only expand to meet the ever-growing demand for greater profits by enlarging their markets, but because they are competing with one another price reductions and their consequent wage cutting is a common tactic. The process may recruit some customers for whom the prices just become payable, but much expansion is at the expense of rival corporations. There are circumstances, like the exploitation of the Nigerian oil-fields or the US battle for Central Asian oil, where corporations will combine to ensure control, but these are usually temporary or sectoral alliances which only occasionally extend into the market-place. Combination may also occur in moments of dramatic price decline, again oil provides examples. During the second half of 1998, its price was at its lowest for over twenty years, particularly in early December when it fell to below US$10 per barrel. That price was lower in real terms than it had been immediately prior to the decision, in 1973, by the Organisation of Petroleum Exporting Countries (OPEC) substantially to increase world prices for crude oil. Profits for the oil companies declined correspondingly and, in order to maintain their market value, many of the largest began to combine, hence, for example, the mergers between Exxon and Mobil and between Total and Petrofina. Economies of scale and consequent increases in profitability have followed – even though part of the price has been paid by redundant workers.[41] In the second half of 1999 and early in 2000, oil prices increased again, but to a point where one analyst remarked that it 'was likely to prove no more sustainable that $10 had been'.[42] By March, reports of a possible reprise of the effects of the 1973 price increases, which upset the financial markets so badly, began to circulate.[43] That upset, like most others on the financial markets, led to considerable privations for those least able to bear them.

Until very recently the world had proved to be large enough for TNCs to find adequate markets without having to trouble too much about the vast populations of the excluded. Now that currency spec-ulation and futile over-production frequently sends finance capital scurrying for cover it is just possible that TNC directors may recall that nineteenth-century British experience and consider ways of extending their reach among the poorer people of the world. It was this hope that buoyed up the now virtually forgotten Commission on Global Governance (1992–95), a successor to the Brandt Commission (1977–80) and chaired jointly by Ingvar Carlsson and Shridath ('Sonny') Ramphal. The Commission's report addressed what it saw as the main problems in governance which could not simply be solved by the separate powers and initiatives of nation states.[44] It considered the place of existing 'institutions of global governance' like the UN, the Bretton Woods organisations and others, including among them the major TNCs.

Corporate power is such that the Commission was unquestionably right to think of the corporations as instruments of global governance and we cannot dispute their view that: 'In some cases, governance will rely primarily on markets and market instruments, perhaps with some institutional oversight.'[45] There are numerous barriers to the emergence of a benign system of global governance, including unabated hegemonic assertions by the world's remaining super-power, arms races and trades, the rise of civil conflict and the growth of violence; but the Commission seems not to have noticed the degree to which TNCs are implicated in all of them. US muscle is normally deployed in support of its commercial interests, manufacturing sophisticated weapons is largely a TNC preserve. International banks have been deeply involved in, for instance, the murderous Serbian regime and in the Afghanistan war. The protection of company pipelines in, among other places, Nigeria and Colombia has been accompanied by TNC-supported violence. Perhaps these and countless other examples account, in a later comment in the Report, for the slight air of nervousness, not to say downright confusion:

Another ... sector with a role in global governance is global business ... we noted the enlarged scale and much more international scope of private enterprise, with some of the larger transnational firms dwarfing the majority of national economies. There is today much wider acceptance of private enterprise and of the benefits of a competitive market system. There remains a need, none the less, to avoid excessive concentration of economic power in private hands, and to have the state protect the public through antitrust or competition policies.

Business must be encouraged to act responsibly ... There are signs that this community is beginning to respond to the opportunities to exercise such responsibility ...

The international community needs to enlist the support of transnational business in global governance and to encourage best practices, acknowledging the role the private sector can play in meeting the needs of the global neighbourhood. Wider acceptance of these responsibilities is likely if the business sector is drawn in to participate in the processes of governance.[46]

Mocking the Commission for its excessively sanguine views would be easy, particularly with the recent and shining example of the world's largest banana firm, Chiquita, dismissing its grossly underpaid Honduran plantation workers shortly after their homes, infrastructure and societies had been destroyed by one of the world's worst hurricanes.[47] But the Commission was struggling to come to terms with a sort of reality, unable, because of its origins and remit, to engage in wholesale criticisms of existing powers. Since TNCs operate globally we can, up to a point, agree to see them as central institutions of global governance; the difference between our position and that of the Commission is that we see corporations as inevitably institutions of bad governance, a characteristic arising from their inherent instability caused by the pursuit of their principal purpose – the enhancement of private profit through competition. However, it does not necessarily follow that worldwide activity means that the acting institution is global.

Panitch has made the point that corporations are not the principal instruments of globalisation, that function belongs to nation states and the arrangements they make between themselves for 'the rules governing capital movements, investment, currency exchange and trade'.[48] States, he argues, remain integral to economies even as they adjust to new economic demands by ensuring that their rules and institutions remain responsive to the changing demands of international trade, but also by 'regulating social actors and markets'. Collaboration between nation states is also required if 'the necessary international juridical and infrastructural conditions for global capital accumulation are [to be] established and maintained'. We may set this alongside the view, offered by Harvey, that the power exercised by TNCs and the financial institutions which support and surround them 'has meant the destruction, invasion, and restructuring of socially constituted places on an unprecedented scale'; he includes in this destruction 'even whole nation states'.[49] Harvey sees the increasing centralisation of this power in some sense as supra-territorial, concentrated in what he describes as a place of difference. The destruction of 'socially constituted spaces', particularly of nation states, is a complex process, seen most obviously in Central Asia and Africa, which unquestionably includes financial globalisation and free-market pressures among its causes. It would, however, be rash to imagine that these pressures stand alone.

One central element in our depressing picture of contemporary capital acquisition is, of course, the role of that increasingly imperialistic state, the USA. Clinton, supported in his terrorist action against Iraq only by Blair, his British myrmidon, may well have been killing a number of foreign civilians and a few soldiers to distract attention from his domestic problems, but the raids also fit well into the US determination to control oil production in the Gulf and in Central Asia. This determination is accompanied by efforts to control oil elsewhere. The bulk of Angola's production, for example, already goes to the US and recently Bangladesh has been bullied by US diplomats attempting to force an agreement to the exploitation of its fossil fuels by US corporations.[50] Simultaneously, partly because of its long-standing and enormous trade deficit, protectionism is a perennial temptation for the US administration. Despite this, it rushes to the defence of its own corporations at the first sign of any foreign attempt at limitation. Europe made a half-hearted gesture towards Caribbean banana production, giving producers some small preferential access to European markets; Chiquita, with its sudden donation of US$500,000 to the Democratic Party's funds, succeeded in getting the issue to the WTO within twenty-four hours of the European ruling.[51] Oil and bananas stand, of course, simply as examples of a far more widespread and determined imperialism.

This may be seen most clearly in the battles surrounding the MAI, which, if it finally comes to be, will bind the signatory nations of the WTO. Joseph K. Roberts has provided a useful summary of the Agreement's specific conditions.[52] These cover unconditional access for exports and services in all signatory states; the free movement of investment capital and the freedom of investors from any signatory state to purchase and, if they wish, remove any industrial or commercial plant; the right to resource extraction with no corresponding duty of maintenance; the right to take profits and to repatriate them to the investor's state and the right of investors to arrange credit in host countries with no regard to its effects on their domestic economies. Investors, most of whom are based within the OECD countries, may purchase any privatised infrastructure without restrictions protecting the rights of citizens; foreign investors are to be given the same grants, loans and tax concessions as all domestic businesses; no demands by governments for domestic employment, domestic purchase or mutual import agreements may be levied; all national agreements (as opposed to a WTO-wide agreement, should it ever exist) protecting human and workers' rights or the environment would become illegal. Sections of the Agreement will prevent any signatory government from introducing new legislation which does not conform with its provisions and will compel the rescinding of existing law. Roberts makes the point that under the terms of the MAI, the court of the investor will hear any challenges; since most of the greatest investors are US corporations other states will be faced with the monumental task of fighting in the developed world's slowest, most arcane, expensive and deeply conservative, neo-liberal courts. It should scarcely need remarking that appropriating the central court of commercial justice is the ultimate seal of empire.

This outrageous agreement, formed on the agenda of US transnationals, was put together in quite remarkable secrecy by the OECD and not until late in the day were its conditions made public. Little or no consultation with electors took place, but interest groups (INGOs in particular) have, in the last few years, managed to mount some opposition and the progress of the MAI has been intermittent. In December 1998, the Agreement was abandoned by the OECD[53] and taken over, with little publicity, by the WTO. That organisation's Third Ministerial Conference ended in the famous 'Battle of Seattle', but not in the defeat of the MAI, merely its postponement. We should not underestimate the impetus behind it; the OECD, in its earlier propaganda document in support of the Agreement, pointed out that 'From 1973–96, FDI flows multiplied fourteen times from $25 billion to $350 billion per annum, outstripping growth in international trade.'[54] So long as free-market orthodoxy remains politically powerful, then arranging matters to suit investment along the lines of the rules of the WTO will be high on the intergovern-mental agendas of the richer social-democratic states. Just as the GATT negotiators dressed up the establishment of the WTO with the spurious argument that its rules would create the conditions neces-sary for fair trade between patently unequal trading nations, so we find the OECD and WTO both engaged in similarly preposterous cant. The policy document, to which we have already referred, quotes the WTO's view that the lack of FDI in poor countries is symptomatic of their poverty rather than its cause. We may feel that this is a breathtaking over-simplification, but we may also judge better of its ambivalence, if not its disingenuity, when, a few para-graphs later, it justified the OECD as the forum for the development of the MAI by pointing out that 'OECD Members have a major stake in investment rules, accounting for 85 per cent of FDI outflows and 60 per cent of inflows.' An argument which is as credible for the WTO as it was for the OECD. Roberts makes the further point that 'seventy-five per cent of FDI is in Europe, North America and Japan'.[55] It is ludicrous to suggest that impoverished and deeply indebted states will be enabled to invest their way out of poverty, or that substantial inward investment would come to their rescue and the continuing annual record of investment speaks for itself (see table 4.1). Our short table, while illustrating a general point, conceals other important issues. Of the 109 economies categorised by the World Bank as being of low to middle (including 'upper-middle') income, just thirteen states received more than the equivalent of US$1 billion in 1996 and, between them, accounted for 29 per cent of the total FDI for 1996.[56] A further four states received between US$500,000 and US$1 billion, a little below 1 per cent.[57] If FDI into high-income countries, including members of the OECD, is taken into account, then it can be seen that the remaining ninety-two states received somewhat under 8 per cent of the total. Many poor countries join the WTO in the fond hope of improving their trading and inward investment positions, others have been pushed into joining by pressure from the World Bank and the IMF. If the MAI, or some similar agreement, is adopted by the WTO, then weaker member states will have no choice but to accept it. Platitudinous and conveniently vague clauses supposedly addressed, like those in GATT's Marrakesh Agreement, to the difficulties facing impoverished states, will probably be included, but no agreement is likely to do anything for them, either in trade or in investment, other than making the foreign exploitation of such resources as they possess even easier than it is at present. It is not without relevance to the entire question to point out that negotiations within the European Round Table of Industrialists (ERT) are in progress for the piecemeal construction of a free-trade agreement between the US and the EU.[58] Quite apart from introducing to European tables that wonder of chemical science the US is pleased to call beef, such an agreement will reinforce the progress of the MAI.

Table 4.1   Comparative figures for FDI, 1970–96

Country group	Annual value of flows (US$ millions) Totals			percentage share[1]		
	1970	1980	1996	1970	1980	1996
Low income	165[2]	1502	9433	0.13	0.78	3.00
Middle income	1467[3]	22185	109341	1.15	11.55	34.70
Low and middle of which:	1632	23687	118774	1.28	12.33	37.70
East Asia & Pacific		10347	58681		5.40	18.60
Europe & Central Asia	n/a[4]	1097	14755		0.57	4.70
Latin America & Caribbean		8188	38015		4.27	12.01
Middle East & North Africa		2757	614		1.44	0.20
South Asia		464	3439		0.24	1.09
Sub-Saharan Africa		834	3271		0.43	1.04
High income	n/a[4]	167908	195922	98.72	87.67	62.30
Total	128000[5]	191595	314696			

1 Discrepancies caused by rounding up.
2 Figure includes disinvestment in Zambia to the value of US$297 million.
3 Figure includes disinvestment in Bolivia, Philippines, Peru, Chile and Venezuela to a total of US$273 million.
4 Figures not provided in World Bank, 1992.
5 Figure taken from Elson, in Corbridge, 1995.

Source: World Bank, *World Development Report, 1992* and *1998/99*

Unregulated financial adventures, gross neo-liberal competition for markets, unregulated trade and a prolonged campaign for equally unregulated investment are, so to say, the background noise to contemporary popular economic thought. Voices, like those of Cole and his fellows, are raised in the wilderness against this barrage, but they lack political power, particularly in the face of unremitting propaganda from the World Bank.[59] Advocacy for free-market policies has been central to the Bank's public statements for decades and it has continued it even when dealing with other major issues confronting the world. The 'Overview' in the *World Development Report, 1992*, for example, is devoted to environmental issues, nevertheless it repeats a prescription offered in the 1991 Report which included 'a set of 'market-friendly' policies for development'. A properly functioning free market, in the Bank's view, would lead to a widespread increase in

> economic activity [which] can cause environmental problems but can also, with the right policies and institutions, help address them ... When individuals no longer have to worry about day-to-day survival, they can devote resources to profitable investments in conservation ... Some problems initially worsen but then improve as incomes rise.[60]

In other words, once everyone has made enough money, some attention might be paid to environmental problems created by the process. Nowhere does the Bank suggest a level of, for instance, GDP which might signal the diversion of some gains to what are essentially social needs. Nor, of course, does it offer any suggestions for policies when large sections of the free market collapse. In 1995, when the warning signs of coming collapse were fairly obvious,[61] the *World Development Report*, in an astonishingly triumphalist 'Overview', remarked that:

> The benefits enjoyed by labor in fast growing economies are not the result of job creation in the public sector or wage increases mandated by government. Expanding employment opportunities and rising wages are the consequences of growth and economy-wide increases in output per worker. A market-based development strategy achieves these outcomes through investment decisions by firms, households, and government.[62]

Note the envoi, further weakening the importance of national governments by that judiciously placed comma.

In 1997, a year in which a little modesty in claims for the ability of free markets to solve all problems might have been expected, we find the annual Report urging the development of national policies which will buttress market structures and help their imagined capacity to correct imperfections and imbalances.[63] The Bank, of course, is not only advocating unrestricted free trade, it is one of the more formidable opponents of democracy. Its view that most of the world's difficulties will be overcome by trifling 'corrections' to the market, leaves it struggling to find roles for democratically elected governments. In 1997, as we have observed, it felt that national governments might gainfully be employed in legislating in support of markets. In its Report dated 1998/99 we find an extraordinarily malapert extension of its position:

> The general principle that institutions should act on their comparative strengths suggests that governments should focus on those responsibilities that the private sector is unlikely to shoulder ... governments should concentrate on activities whose spillover effects (externalities) are especially important, that have clear public good characteristics, or that address distributional concerns.[64]

This passage occurs in the course of a polemic about the relationship between knowledge and development. Few would deny such a relationship, but it is, of course, a vacuous concept without a definition of its separate terms. We do not have to look far for those offered by the World Bank, they are expressed very clearly in the course of its unequivocal defence of the Green Revolution and, indirectly, of the activities of the agrichemical corporations.[65] Even more important in understanding the Bank's contempt for democracy, we should recall that during the 1980s and the 1990s the 'tiger economies', whose successes were offered as vindication of the free market and as role models for development, largely emerged in sub-metropolitan states with autocratic or oligarchic, authoritarian governments. In the case of the Celtic tiger, democratic collusion with widespread corporate and political corruption was the key.

That background noise produced by governments, industry, finance and its multiform institutions in their worldwide insistence on the inevitability of the free market for 'progress' has led to the emergence of managerial approaches to capitalism in which the role of the state is seen as one of moderating excesses. This despite the aspirations of the framers of the MAI who would seem altogether to deny the possibility of such excesses. Capital accumulation and the competition on which it is based may have got a little out of hand, but it is, in the view of the moderators, a natural and necessary state of existence in need only of correction by means of widening its ideological focus. Among the most spirited and, indeed, successful of those economists determined not to change but to rectify the system may be counted the members of the London Environmental Economics Centre (LEEC). In particular, two of their publications have been remarkably influential, *Blueprint for a Green Economy* and *Blueprint 2* (other volumes have followed, but none so effective as these). Their authors set out to develop an economics in response, in part, to the IUCN's *World Conservation Strategy*[66] but chiefly followed the Brundtland Report. They saw the latter as showing 'that it is *possible* to achieve a path of economic development for the global economy' in line with its famous definition of sustainability and, of course, in doing so broadly accepted the capitalist economic framework within which Brundtland was working.[67]

Pearce and his fellows share with Will Hutton the neo-Keynesian belief that capital accumulation and competition can, by means of social-democratic consensus, be controlled. It is a valiant conviction, calling for nerves of steel when faced with the actual behaviour of, for example, the interests engaged in the trade in non-traditional agricultural exports (NTAEs) in Sub-Saharan Africa, or in the addictive gambling on the international bourses to which we have already referred. In this scheme other behaviours need also to be modified; social-democrat politicians in particular must be weaned away from their habit of buying votes by redistributing taxation not to socially worthwhile objectives, but to those sectors of the population they feel to be most influential. The *Blueprint* authors are not unaware of these and other difficulties but place their faith in what they feel to be economic good sense – environmentally sustainable development, as it is defined in the Brundtland report, is, they suggest, not only equitable but is also, in the long run, more profitable.

Their method is relatively simple and depends first on understanding 'the value of natural, built and cultural environments', the
importance of long-term views (the lifetime of our grandchildren is
the common, if uncertain, measure) and the need for some degree of
equity. 'Resources' and 'wealth' become more or less interchangeable
terms and the authors distinguish between 'capital wealth ... the
stock of all man made things' and 'natural wealth or ... capital ... the
stock of environmentally given assets such as soil and forest, wildlife
and water'.[68] We need not quibble with 'environmentally given', nor
with 'the stock of all man made things' since the meanings are made
quite plain as the argument in both books proceeds. There are
obvious ideological objections to defining everything, including
human labour, as resources or capital assets, but we may temporarily
leave them aside while discussing the LEEC's position. The distinction
here is between what is commonly and relatively easily valued in a
balance sheet and what, so far, has evaded such capture. Most
resources have owners, but those without, like the greater part of the
world's seas or the atmosphere, are defined as 'open access'
resources.[69] In this discourse the environment itself veers uneasily
between being a resource and an ill-defined agglomerate of both
capital and natural wealth. Pearce and his co-authors see environmental damage and its consequent social effects as springing, at least
in part, from the exclusion of common goods, 'open access resources',
from the pricing process. Because they are 'free', neither their use nor
their pollution or destruction have a market value. Since they cannot
be included in a balance sheet, manufacturers and other decision
makers may, unless prevented piecemeal by public *force majeure*, use,
damage, even destroy, these resources at will. It is, therefore, essential
to construct a means of giving monetary values to open access
resources and including them in *pricing* goods and services.[70]

Blueprint for a Green Economy began its life as a report prepared for
the British Government's Department of the Environment and it is
important to recognise that it was accepted during the Prime
Ministership of Margaret Thatcher, an ideologically extremist free
marketeer. Although the book takes notional free-market trading as
the context of its arguments and, indeed, as the fulcrum for one
central proposal, the authors give the overall impression of being unre-
constructed Keynesian redistributionists. Early in the book they
advance the view that equity, 'providing for the needs of the least

advantaged in society ("intragenerational equity"), and ... fair treatment of future generations ("intergenerational equity")',[71] is one of
the essential means of achieving sustainable development. When they
come to deal with equity more thoroughly, they pose the question:
'What is the justification for ensuring that the next generation has at
least as much wealth ... as this one?'[72] Rephrased it could also include
intragenerational equity and it is clear from the book as a whole that
such an inclusion was intended, but it is a question that the authors
do not answer. Instead, they describe the concepts involved in the
process, yet the moral, even the economic imperative, if such exists,
would seem to be called for by the use of the word 'justification' and
the problem is not addressed. In a sense this charge is unfair since, in
their Preface, the authors associate their work with the Brundtland
Report and the positions it adopts. *Our Common Future* is more
cautious and simply argues for a relationship between 'equity and the
common interest'[73] based on largely unadduced evidence for its efficiency. It is possible for us to speculate on whether the auspices under
which the report was produced account for the authors' failure to
address the issue of equality, rather than simply equity of opportunity.

Blueprint 2 concludes with a chapter by R. Kerry Turner entitled
'Environment, Economics and Ethics' in which he briefly analyses the
issues in terms of environmental ethics and finally states that the
authors in this volume are adopting what he calls a 'modified
"extended" CBA [cost-benefit analysis] approach' to intergenerational
equity. It depends on what Kerry Turner calls the 'constant natural
assets rule' in which while 'natural assets' passed on to the future
cannot be identical with those enjoyed at present, they should not be
less in overall value. New discoveries and advances in technology, paid
for in the present, would become part of that future stock. This
involves altering 'the utilitarian cost-benefit paradigm' so as to
compensate 'the future for environmental damage being done now'
which, in turn, depends on 'raising the implicit value of environmental impacts relative to "development"', an objective which means
pricing environmental goods. The chapter ends with the somewhat
circular argument that the authors of this volume and, therefore, of its
predecessor, adopt this approach because, unlike 'preservationist
bioethics paradigm[s]', it works.[74] But the failure to deal with the
question of why the constant natural assets rule should be adopted by
the world of free markets means that the authors offer little with

which to counter the overwhelming tendency of businesses to disregard equity and environmental damage in pursuit of profit. Even more seriously, CBA is hopelessly enmired in a system which equates all value with what is of value to the analyst and to any respondents to analytical enquiry. This becomes a problem of power which will recur with even greater force in our discussion of justice in the next chapter.

Both these books, the second elaborating the first, are admirable examples of that economic thinking which sees the 'market' as the principal and, for the foreseeable future, the athanasian regulator of human exchange, but which also understands the need to polish its rougher edges. They are almost certainly right that capitalism will not suddenly disappear, no matter how acute its crises, but they seem not to have sufficient grasp of its capacity to dissimulate. We may see this in events which we have already mentioned. Thus, with the ignoble exception of Britain's government formed by the meretriciously named New Labour Party, social-democratic regimes throughout the world have enacted a variety of measures designed to protect their shorn lambs from the coldest of market winds. In the eyes of many post-Keynesian economists this is one vital role for nation states and is part of their wider function in creating, as it were, the ring in which TNCs may batter profits out of a largely captive public. We may also see this kind of regulation as a sop for dismantling or co-opting trades unions. But it is by no means clear that trades unionism has completely been defeated and national regulation, weak as much of it is, is still seen by the corporations and their financiers as a barrier to their operations. Inconsistency has always been a characteristic of social-democratic states; we need only think, on the one hand, of its departments of overseas aid fighting for larger and untied aid budgets while its departments of trade and industry, on the other, see aid as an instrument of profit-making in poorer countries. There have, of course, been times when that inconsistency has been an important element in social advance: we may have an example in the shifty response of some governments to what could turn out to be a step in the democratisation of Europe in the January 1999 censure dispute in the European Parliament. One of the most glaring examples of the more dubious effects of inconsistency may be seen in those governments, while regulating to protect their citizens from the worst ravages of the market, are simultaneously creating an agreement (the MAI) which could override their own protective regulation.

These battles bring us to the central weakness in the LEEC's brave proposals, which, it is worth noting, are essentially sophisticated versions of the 'polluter pays' principle. Incorporating environmental and social damage into balance sheets, so that the agents responsible are obliged to meet their 'real' costs, with the object of deterring them from causing the damage in the first place, is open to major criticism. The simplest objection is that no matter what safeguards are proposed, profits will not be permitted substantially to decline and costs will be passed on to the consumer. It is a principle which leaves undisturbed the relationships and priorities of capital and, in particular, does not deal with one of the most irresponsible of polluters, the packaging industry. We have already commented on the trade in pollution licences, it is a trade which will grow to the obvious detriment of poorer states because their industrial development will be inhibited unless the current reluctance of the capitalist world to transfer affordable new technology and aid for the creation of technological cultures is overcome. In the capitalist world poorer people whose environment is, prior to the trade in licences, already seriously polluted, will suffer further as their governments buy in unused quotas from elsewhere. There are a number of other practical and conceptual problems, several of them adverted to by Pearce and his fellows but, so long as the LEEC's central proposition is accepted, then neither these problems, nor the objections we have raised, are impossible to meet.

What really renders the LEEC's programme suspect is that it proposes to commodify 'open access resources' and, in consequence, increases the scope of the definition of people not as social beings, but as customers. It does so in two ways: it expands the function of the balance sheet such that it further encloses what, hitherto, might be called geographical social space (rather like land enclosures); it then sells what it has enclosed – the price being pollution and its social costs – back to those from whom it has appropriated these 'resources' in the first place. Lying at the heart of this process is the *transformation*, the reduction, of environment and social space to 'resources' and is the root of our objection. In the previous chapter we mentioned Harvey's argument against this reductionism. To it, we would add that the consequence of seeing the environment as a collection of resources which should be priced and thus commodified, is to accept, without reservation, a post-Malthusian economic structure as the fundamental basis of human social congress. It is to assent to the principles of that capitalist free-market ideology so succinctly summarised by Thatcher in her demagogic and declamatory dismissal of society; a system that is dependent on the competition that inevitably marginalises or completely excludes so many people. Once again, as an example, we may look at the biochemical corporations (Monsanto, in particular) and their scramble to patent basic elements in the food chain and in biological structure itself. It is, in short, that same totalitarianism of market ideology advocated by the World Bank and its cohorts.

In 1990 Pearce, Barbier and Markandya restated and expanded their general position in another book entitled *Sustainable Development: Economics and Environment in the Third World*. Their first chapter offers a definition of sustainable development which begins by remarking that development 'is a value word, implying change that is *desirable* ... We take development to be a *vector* of desirable social objectives.' Among the list of elements in such a vector they include: increased real per capita incomes, improved health and nutrition, better education, 'access to resources', greater equity in incomes and improvements in basic freedoms. They follow this unexceptional programme with a discussion of what they see as the first condition for sustainable development – 'constant capital stock'.[75] Most of the remainder of the book goes to supporting this assertion – we should not cavil, they are economists firmly within the capitalist tradition.

So far we have, in this chapter, sketched the economic context in which discussions about development must take place. Since it is not possible to escape, in any immediately practical sense, the normative power of capitalism over contemporary economic endeavour, serious questions about economic sustainability present themselves. They are obviously pertinent to INGOs because many of them have experienced practical difficulties in the field consequent on unregulated free-market activity, these problems have resulted in some reassessments of policy. But it is the intellectuals, politicians and NGOs of the ninety-two excluded countries, particularly of those where the state has actually, or virtually, collapsed for whom these questions are acute. If the current market crisis worsens and capital continues to fly from fragile 'tiger' economies, their number may well increase. In earlier chapters we have commented on the globalisation of poverty, what we might dub a 'new geography of poverty', created by unfettered competition; it affects people in the industrialised world as well as in the Third World and is not concealed by vacuous comment about new expectations in life following the disappearance of job security. Extreme poverty is common even in many of the member states of the OECD; for the poor, both old and new, the questions about development, that process which is 'nothing but the perpetuation of the differential rate of exploitation',[76] are also of immediate and pressing importance.

The central question is obvious: in which economic discourse, or framework, are development in general and programmes and projects in particular to be considered economically sustainable? Another form of the question is: who is making the decision that a specific developmental endeavour is economically sustainable and in whose interest? Much of the world's developmental agenda is directly or indirectly dominated by the World Bank and the IMF; both institutions are governed more or less exclusively by the financial ideology common to the banking world. Larry Elliott, writing in the *Guardian*, is a good deal more blunt: 'The system is designed to feed America's consumption habit, with capital liberalisation a way of ensuring the United States has access to the savings of the rest of the world. Only that way can it finance its burgeoning current account deficit.'[77] This excellent and angry article *inter alia* raises the issue of the dangerous balance of payments deficit in the US economy. It is a substantial element in the not wholly improbable danger of a collapse in the US stock market (Elliott has frequently discussed this issue in his newspaper), an event which would have cataclysmic effects on the world's poor and would dramatically increase their number. To illustrate the centrality of our question about the control of economic discourse we may consider the case of Haiti which offers a good, if depressing, example of the issues.

Haiti is roughly twice the size of the six counties of Northern Ireland and its population was estimated, in 1995, to be just over seven million[78] – almost four-and-a-half times that of the British enclave in Ireland. One of the twenty poorest countries in the world, it is also one of the most environmentally devastated; these phenomena are not unrelated.[79] In 1492, an ominous year for so many people beyond Europe's shores, Columbus had claimed for the Spanish crown an island in the Caribbean known to its people as

Quizqueya and renamed it La Isla Española. Its large population of Arawak people were subsequently virtually wiped out by a mix of new diseases, forced labour and genocidal slaughter. Spanish entre-preneurs, who renamed the island San Domingo, began to replace the original inhabitants by importing a slave population from Africa at the rate of about 20,000 a year. In 1697, following the Treaty of Rijswijk,[80] the western third of the island was ceded by Spain to France. Sugar plantations, which had been established in the coastal plains by slave labour under the Spaniards, were expanded by the French, or, more accurately, by their slaves and, in 1734, they began to cultivate coffee on the lower mountain slopes, leaving the heavily forested mountainous interior (rising to over 3,000 metres) largely untouched. San Domingo (Saint-Domingue to the French) rapidly became France's most valuable possession and one of the richest colonies in the world. The rising of the slaves in 1791, led by Toussaint L'Ouverture and inspired by the French Revolution, its advances and set-backs, and the subsequent creation of the world's first black republic, Haiti, in 1804, is a story glowingly told in the account by C.L.R. James.[81] Slavery collapsed, despite Napoleon Bonaparte's attempts to put the revolution down and to reinstate it. L'Ouverture's successor, Jean-Jacques Dessalines, tried to make himself an 'Emperor', but was assassinated. Spain recovered two thirds of the island under the Treaty of Paris in 1914 and the area of the present republic was determined.

The collapse of slavery meant the collapse, also, of the plantation economy (though not of all the actual plantations) and its gradual replacement, almost uniquely in Latin America, not by *latifundios* or industrial agriculture, but by an economy largely based on peasant smallholdings. Leaders of the revolution and the few relatively well-to-do people of mixed race moved into commerce and became the foundation of the subsequent urban élite. With each new generation smallholdings were further divided, compelling more and more smallholders to clear forest in the foothills of the mountains for cultivation. Much of the land was devoted to subsistence farming, but increasing numbers of farmers used parts of their holdings to grow coffee, indigo and cocoa. These crops were sold cheap to urban exporters and sold on by them at enormous profits. That relatively small urban élite grew immensely rich on the trade, the farmers grew increasingly poor. At the same time the young state, itself controlled by the urban rich, increasingly depended on poor peasant tax-payers for its revenue and since little of it was spent on rural welfare or investment, the smallholders and their dependants were doubly exploited. This exploitation fuelled the civil war of 1867 and the political instability and economic crises which followed it.

Haitian business adventurers encouraged foreigners to invest in infrastructural building and in the purchase of sugar plantations, but this led to the substantial repatriation of profits and a consequently deeply unfavourable balance of payments deficit with, chiefly, the US. By the end of the nineteenth century, a number of differing demands increased the pressure on Haiti's forests. Commercial logging, both for mahogany and for other logs, charcoal burning to feed urban woodfuel demand and industrialised sugar refining and rural woodfuel needs were among them. Then, in 1915, the US invaded Haiti because it had failed to redeem its debts to US business and despite heroic resistance led, initially, by Charlemagne Péralte, the US remained in occupation until 1934. Like most imperial powers, the occupiers spent their time extracting what they could from the conquered state and, in the process, increased the pressure on the forests by demanding wood, not only for export, but for further infrastructure to make extraction easier; they also took control of over 100,000 hectares of agricultural land, dispossessing thousands of peasants. Their greatest crime was the introduction of mass forced-labour overseen by the army – effectively the reintro-duction of slavery. When they were finally persuaded to leave, their dependent Haitian élite began a long series of struggles for power characterised by constant coups and counter-coups and culminating in the notorious dictatorship, backed by the US, of 'Papa Doc' Duvalier. Port-au-Prince, Haiti's capital, became ever larger, swollen by, among others, the dispossessed, and its demands on woodfuel correspondingly increased. Duvalier's rapacious regime eventually produced an armed reaction. Among the measures he took in his attempts at defeating it was to raze further substantial areas of a rapidly declining forest in the fond hope of denying guerrillas cover. 'Papa Doc' died in 1971 and was succeeded by his equally viperous son, Jean-Claude, known widely as 'Baby Doc'.

Matters, by the 1980s, were very serious: of Haiti's population, then around six million, four-and-a-half million were peasants living on holdings rarely much more than one hectare; it was estimated that 75 per cent of them were living on severely degraded land and on the edge of starvation. Kleptocratic governments, backed by the US, remained in power, but solutions to the major problems had to be found. Unsurprisingly, what became popularly known as the 'American Plan' was instituted and was a reaffirmation of free-market principles: Haiti, it was suggested, should trade upon its strengths, the greatest of which was cheap labour. The United States' Agency for International Development (USAID) promoted a substantial number of light industries, mainly assembly plants, owned by US companies in a scheme mimetic of Mexico's *maqiladora* factories. In rural areas, US investment was encouraged in farming for the export market. But the final collapse of the Duvaliers' ensanguined dictatorship in 1986[82] made possible the sudden emergence of previously underground '[o]rganisations of peasants, slum dwellers, students and workers [who] saw the US approach as part of a plan to make Haiti economically dependent on its northern neighbour'. In rural areas peasant movements began to organise 'cooperatives, credit systems, and takeovers of idle or stolen land'[83] and to introduce improved crop storage methods; they also began reforestation and crucial agro-forestry, soil preservation and land-reform programmes. Effectively two rival schemes for the regeneration of Haiti had come to be. The former was backed by the US, the latter received some small encouragement from the reform of land-law in the post-Duvalier regimes.

In December 1990 a socially conscious priest, Jean-Baptiste Aristide, won the elections as leader of the National Front for Change and Democracy. He was subsequently censured by his ecclesiastical superiors and expelled from his religious order (the Salesians) for his interpretation of Liberation Theology – the ideology from which he drew his justification for the war against corruption and drug trafficking, the promotion of literacy and his campaign to move from abject poverty to 'poverty with dignity'. He was deposed by a bloody military coup in September 1991 led by General Raoul Cédras, a more conservative kind of Catholic. One of the conditions of Aristide's return, in 1994, negotiated on Governor's Island in New York and brokered by the US, was that the Haitian government should enter into an agreement with the IMF. A structural adjustment programme was to be installed in which any state-run enterprises would be privatised, import tariffs removed and, most importantly, exports would be promoted. This was clearly disastrous for the peasants and their organisations whose economic discourse ran entirely counter to the extractive and socially destructive policies of the IMF. It is in this context that we return to our question: in which economic discourse, or framework, are development in general and programmes and projects in particular to be considered economically sustainable? Haiti cannot meet its debt repayments or return to profitability in the capitalist sense unless it accepts the IMF's shackles – we may leave aside the issue of whether it could do so even if it accepted the entire IMF–World Bank package happily. USAID, working through the Pan-American Development Foundation (PADF) and the Cooperative Agency for Relief Everywhere (CARE), has made uncomprehending gestures in the direction of reforestation, but confined its activities to farms owned privately by the wealthier peasants.[84] In an interview given in 1995, Chavannes Jean-Baptiste reported that 'even in PADF's own evaluation eighty to ninety per cent of these trees don't survive'.[85] A successful peasant economy is plainly impossible without the reforms and activities promoted by the peasant movements, but the financial big guns are in the hands of those who see such movements as, at best, irrelevant and, at worst, subversive.

Conflicts between differing accounts of economic sustainability could scarcely be illustrated more starkly, but the issue becomes even more acute. Development workers entering a country or region dominated by an IMF–World Bank strategy must recognise that, for many people, changing their priorities so as to conform with that strategy may seem to be the only sensible option. Alternative economic accounts, like those inherent in the plans of the Haitian peasant organisations, entail exactly the environmentally sound procedures endorsed by most INGO thinking and, in the long run, are far more stable. Nevertheless, where capitalist finance and production are dominant, the more effective economic solutions are likely to fail – to be made, in short, 'unsustainable'. All the opportunities have been legally monopolised.

Throughout this chapter we have argued that very specific economic choices have been made by corporations and their client states which are directed towards the perpetual maximisation and growth of profit. The production of goods and services for consumption and exchange is subordinated to the production of finance capital. This has resulted in the extraordinary phenomenon of mass redundancies in times of economic recovery, for example, the Deutscher Bank and the Dresdner Bank recently announced a merger and have been quite open in saying that the consequent boost in profits would be at the cost of 16,000 jobs. The merger subsequently collapsed, but not on the ground of saving those jobs. Andy Merrifield of the Graduate School of Geography, Clark University, in an excellent account of this process, quoted a report from the *New York Times* (3 March 1996):

> More than 43 million jobs have been erased in the United States since 1979 ... Nearly three-quarters of all households have had a close encounter with layoffs since 1980 ... While permanent layoffs have been symptomatic of most recessions, now they are occurring in the same large numbers even during an economic recovery that has lasted five years and even at companies that are doing well.

Merrifield points out that discarding large parts the workforce springs from two related causes. Accumulation demands fierce 'fratricidal' competition between companies and costs may be reduced by reductions in the workforce; but this competition also leads to the concentration and centralisation of the process of accumulation (which may be observed in the German banks) described by Marx.[86] The perennial competitive struggle for greater and greater profit is anarchical, unstable and intensely socially destructive because the costs are always borne by an exploited and discardable workforce. That substantial part of the world's population fighting, often unsuccessfully, to be incorporated in that process because it seems better than increasingly threatened subsistence farming, is of even less interest to capital and its markets than the workers they dismiss.

Huge numbers of jobs become casual because the costs of such labour is lower than maintaining a staff. Casualisation is also a means by which private capital can absorb public assets in those states, like Britain, with a sufficiently complaisant government. Hospital care in the NHS offers an example: in the past, hospital ward cleaners also helped in the business of keeping sick patients clean, in providing them with some company and in the general running of their wards. Cleaning was privatised and contract cleaners took over; it was then discovered that patients occupied beds for longer periods and that recovery rates were both lower and slower. What the cleaners provided in terms of human contact and other *ad hoc* services was an important element in recovery. The end result has been the creation of a body of nursing auxiliaries to supply those services beyond simple cleaning originally provided by the permanently employed cleaners. A substantial part of the NHS, the cleaning, has thus been turned over to the production of corporate profit and the costs for replacing the *ad hoc* but essential 'value added' by full-time cleaners, have actually increased. Perversely, the lesson drawn from this, particularly by New Labour, has been understood to endorse the move towards privatisation.

We have said that the economic pressures that batten on and produce poverty are the consequences of specific political choices, not of some inexorable law of nature. Such choices are obviously an issue, not only for politics, but also for social justice. In the next chapter we shall look at what we mean by justice and the bodies of law on which it is founded.

5
Si Quid Usquam Iustitia
('If there is justice anywhere', Virgil, *Aeneid*, Bk 1)

Reinhold Niebuhr once remarked that 'justice makes democracy possible'.[1] His aphorism is, of course, subject to criticisms similar to those we have offered in the preceding chapters – 'justice' and 'democracy' are as polysemic as any other abstraction. Socrates made the point about justice nearly two-and-a-half millennia ago, particularly in his dialogue with Polemarchus.[2] Yet the present authors begin from the proposition that sustainability can mean nothing unless development is socially just. Indeed, it is our pleonasm; if development is not socially just, then it is not, since suitably qualified we consider it to be a virtue, development. We are familiar enough with injustice, it lies in the poverty and political repression engendered by 'capital's order of social metabolic reproduction' to which we have been devoting this book. Difficulties arise precisely in determining what political and philosophical assumptions we make in our ontological summation of social justice, since, outside professional legal and philosophical circles, what is 'just' is largely either taken for granted or thought to be self-evident. To a considerable degree, questions about justice in Western society have involved an ethical debate which is, itself, heavily dependent on the individualism inherent in much post-Cartesian philosophy. For this reason we have adopted, in this chapter, an approach to the concept founded on law. Although laws may be just or unjust and may, themselves, be subject to the determinations of justice, they are the framework on which justice hangs. Laws are simultaneously the product of decisions about justice and the conditions which most modify our conception of it.

Before we examine the central argument about the foundation of law and, hence, our concept of justice, we must consider briefly a contemporary debate which serves only to muddy the waters. Many disenchanted theorists of development, particularly among INGOs, are formulating an account of society in which the state is contrasted with 'civil society'. The latter is seen as a natural defence against sometimes ill-defined but always menacing encroachments of the former and particularly against unjust law. In our view, the argument has occurred as a response to the neo-liberal harnessing of the state to the interests of global finance and takes the form it does in order to evade the consequences of a necessary political confrontation. But its value as a serious foundation for extra-governmental action is largely unexamined and would, if it were successful, reduce our ability to battle for international social justice. In the nineteenth century, this concept of civil society was adopted by Pierre-Joseph Proudhon[3] and bitterly attacked by Karl Marx. Part of the latter's argument is summarised in one of his letters:

> What is society, whatever its form may be? The product of men's reciprocal action. Are men free to choose this or that form of society? By no means. Assume a particular state of development in the productive faculties of man and you will get a particular form of commerce and consumption. Assume particular stages of development in production, commerce and consumption and you will have a corresponding social constitution, a corresponding organisation of the family, of orders or of classes, in a word, a corresponding civil society. Assume a particular civil society and you will get particular political conditions which are only the official expression of civil society. M. Proudhon will never understand this because he thinks he is doing something great by appealing from the state to civil society – that is to say, from the official résumé of society to official society.[4]

Marx repeatedly returned to this issue in his accounts of the bourgeoisie. Examples may be found in, among other texts, *The Manifesto of the Communist Party*, *The Critique of the Gotha Programme* and, most significantly, right at the beginning of his introduction to the

Grundrisse[5] – significant because he sees it as central to an understanding of 'material production'.

Civil society, as it is discussed among professionals in development (both domestic and overseas) is offered as an alternative to the repressive, or the merely uninterested, state. It is thought to comprise those institutions of goodwill, primarily NGOs of one sort or another, including churches and the like, which will provide either an alternative ideology or an alternative means of acting which will stand between the state and its people. In extreme cases, as in heavily repressive states, or at least in those lacking the ability absolutely to control their people, civil society is often seen as the embryonic form of new governance. In these cases INGOs and development theorists tend to work, so far as possible, with and through these groups. If, as has frequently been the case, 'civil society' does come to power in such states, its international supporters commonly look on with dismay as the new state relapses into the unfortunate habits of the old. We need think only of Indonesia, Malaysia or Zimbabwe for examples. Disappointment, which is even more acute for those who lose out in those transformations from colonialism, arises not because it was wrong or mistaken to support indigenous groups, but because the frustrated hope was pinned to a false distinction.

Latter-day Proudhonists have not understood the circularity of what Mészáros calls 'capital's second order mediations'. These are the norms of bourgeois society: the nuclear family, the means of production, money and the way in which it works, the identification of human needs with the acquisition of particular products (Marx called it 'the fetishism of the commodity'[6]), labour by those without the power to own or control the means of production, the variety of ways in which capital creates states which encounter each other as nation states and, finally, 'the uncontrollable *world market*'.[7] The dynamics of these factors are mutually supportive and are collectively so ravelled that any opposition attempting some alleviation of major social ills finds itself ultimately incapable of overcoming what seem to be infrangible sets of linkages. In differing degrees this holds true for both rich and poor states. Following World War II many of the wealthier countries introduced emancipatory social legislation and welfare structures specifically designed to prevent the recurrence of those excesses of capital which had caused so much misery in the years before the war. New institutions, like the British National

Health Service and its equivalents elsewhere, or like enhanced educational structures, subsidised public transport, moderately progressive taxation and so on, seemed to form the basis of a compromise which at least guaranteed a measure of social justice for the fortunate inhabitants of some developed democracies. With the advent of monetarism, the reintroduction of unbridled *laissez-faire* and the reassertion of those capitalist norms, that compromise and its moderating institutions are being rudely smashed. It would not be unreasonable to see this phenomenon as an object lesson in the futility of the Proudhonist position. In this discourse distinctions between the state and civil society are merely fanciful.[8]

Our purpose here is only to consider the delusions of reformers within the central states of capitalism and not to advance an argument for refusing to support indigenous socio-political movements created by the world's poor. The post-World War II compromise in much of the industrialised world did little to address the problems of poor states but, when thought was given to them at all, it was widely supposed that with sufficient goodwill and some small financial effort, such benefits could be extended worldwide. Many of the international enquiries into the difficulties of poor states and their people, culminating in the Brandt Reports[9] and the Brundtland Report, have, among their underlying assumptions, the proposition that structurally developmental models should be based on the norms of social democracy. In other words, allowing for some cultural differences, the object of any concern or any aid is to help poor countries to 'develop' into capitalist clones. We have been at pains, in the last chapter, to show why this ambition is impossible to achieve and can only entrap these states further in their position as exploited clients of the industrialised states and of the global institutions of financial and commercial governance.

Not only is that ambition unachievable, its propriety is also open to some doubt, particularly given the polysemy of 'justice'. Part of the unpacking of our 'ontological summation of social justice', must be a brief look at what is formally meant by 'justice'. It will allow us to exclude some things which tend confusingly to be rolled into any wider account. We may begin with divine justice, which is commonly based on some sort of synoptic list of exhortations and prohibitions, at least among the world's major religions; the Ten Commandments, for example, is a rudimentary moral code. Divine justice is about determining just deserts – rewards or punishments – for those who excel and for those who fall short of its tenets. What lies at the root of such systems, apart from claims to some epiphanic origin, is a moral philosophy which offers a sort of mathematical interconnectedness between *is* and *ought*.[10] Since religious systems are rarely divorced entirely from the societies in which they operate, they commonly extend their moral codes to issues of social organisation. We may consider the eccentrically variable social dicta from successive Popes,[11] or the vagaries of social control, all introduced in the name of Islam, following the Ayatollah Ruhollah Khomeini's revolution in Iran (1979). A good example is the *fatwa* condemning Salman Rushdie. Even a cursory acquaintance with Islam makes clear to any reader of *Satanic Verses* that his 'crime' was not blasphemy but satire – the one medium that can terrify a theocracy. Divine justice, despite parallels in secular systems, cannot form part of our account, not the least because it is authenticated by some variously identified non-human power to whom only the elect have access.

Society, of course, has its own equivalent of religious moral law in its concept of retributive justice; underlying its administration is a complex of philosophical arguments dealing with the ethics and fittingness of punishment for the acts which it judges to be criminal. There are obvious ways in which this relates to social justice and, as Nietzsche pointed out, 'punishment is clearly overlaid with all sorts of uses'.[12] High among them is its function in elaborating what we might call both the 'theatre' and the mechanisms of social control, but it also functions as a reflection of social norms – not so much in the ways that retribution is constructed, but more in terms of what sort of activity appears as crime at any given time in response to normative social conditions. Thus Michel Foucault made the point:

> In the second half of the eighteenth century … with the general increase in wealth, but also with the sudden demographic expansion, the principal target of popular illegality tended to be not so much rights, as goods: pilfering and theft tended to replace smuggling and the armed struggle against the tax agents.[13]

Foucault's *Discipline and Punish* is a social-historical and philosophical disquisition on the use of imprisonment in reinforcing social norms and its adaptation as an instrument of retribution as each society creates its own special forms of crime. Retributive justice is overwhelmingly concerned with ways to 'let the punishment fit the crime',[14] and at least one philosopher has pointed to the ways in which this happens, 'fines are like theft, imprisonment like kidnapping, etc.',[15] consequently it is also primarily concerned with defining what is criminal. Despite its cousinship with social justice, which may be said to be even closer than that of divine justice, retributive justice is also outside our immediate concern.[16]

We have spelt out our exclusion of these two discourses in justice from our discussion because many practitioners and theorists in development and humanitarian assistance, including the present authors, make judgements using language appropriate to both.[17] In suggesting that the chief measure of sustainability in development must be that it is socially just, we are also operating within the confines of bourgeois social thinking. Yet, no matter what our criticisms of that thinking may be, we must examine existing phenomena – development programmes – in terms of the political and philosophical categories within which they operate. Socially just development is largely a matter, in existing forms of judicial analysis, of distributive justice, which might crudely be described as concerning the ethics of the distribution of benefits and responsibilities or burdens. Obviously this should include the distribution of the means of production as well as consumption, but it is an issue rarely examined in this debate. Equity, in the sense of '[t]he quality of being equal or fair; fairness, impartiality; even-handed dealing',[18] rather than the jurisprudential meaning of a body of law recognised in England, Ireland and the USA, lies behind many of the concepts included in distributive justice. It means that people who are similarly placed in their basic needs should be similarly treated.[19] Gender and racial equality are, in theory, subsumed under this rubric. Attractive in its simplicity, this position begs the questions of who is treating whom and what counts as need. Other problems appear because people are obviously and massively unequally situated and the issue rapidly becomes the invidious process of determining tolerable levels of inequity. In considering the contemporary question of socially just and thus sustainable development, we are frequently ensnared by that process.

It is an argument which surfaces in much contemporary writing in the philosophy of law, particularly since the publication of *A*

Theory of Justice by John Rawls.[20] In that immensely influential work, Rawls sets out to generalise and carry 'to a higher level of abstraction the familiar theory of the social contract as found, say, in Locke, Rousseau and Kant'. He begins by proposing that the 'principles of justice' are what 'free and rational persons concerned to further their own interests would accept in an initial position of equality as defining the fundamental terms of their association'. This approach will result in what he calls 'justice as fairness'. He remarks that the ahistorical 'initial position of equality' corresponds to the state of nature in theories of social contract. Rawls proposes another hypothetical position which he terms 'the veil of ignorance', in which none of the 'free and rational persons', in determining the legal arrangements which make up their terms of association, have any knowledge of their class, possessions, abilities and so on. Only thus would fairness be ensured.[21] We shall deal more fully with this understanding later in this chapter, but our difficulties with it are probably obvious, since they spring from our rejection of idealist philosophy. What Rawls struggled for in this book and developed more fully in later work,[22] was, primarily, a basis for criticising existing unfair law. This view is reinforced by his assertion that benevolence, in asserting the needs of others, is unnecessary if the mutual disinterestedness of the original position is combined with the veil of ignorance.[23] He neglects to remark that benevolence, unlike some works of supererogation (which he also deals with in the passage we have quoted from *A Theory of Justice*) commonly arises from a position of power.

In an elaboration of Rawls's theory, Brian Barry[24] has proposed two 'constructivist' theories of justice: one of them, which is widely held and for which he offers strong arguments, he rejects, the other he defends.[25] The first of the two ultimately derives, as Barry points out, from an argument advanced against Socrates, in Plato's *Republic*, by Glaucon:

> It is according to nature a good thing to inflict wrong or injury and a bad thing to suffer it, but that the disadvantages of suffering it exceed the advantages of inflicting it; after a taste of both, therefore, men decide that, as they can't evade the one and achieve the other, it will pay to make a compact with each other by which they forgo both. They accordingly make laws and mutual agree-

ments, and what the law lays down they call lawful and right. This is the origin and the nature of justice. It lies between what is most desirable, to do wrong and avoid punishment, and what is most undesirable, to suffer wrong without being able to get redress; justice lies between these two and is accepted not as being good in itself, but as having a relative value due to our inability to do wrong. For anyone who had the power to do wrong and was a real man would never make any such agreement with anyone – he would be mad if he did.[26]

Although Socrates dismisses it, Barry remarks that Plato regarded this argument as the most serious on offer in opposition to Socrates' view which, since it depends on arguments about the arrangement of the human soul, Barry does not discuss. Glaucon's argument may be summarised thus: it is in the interests of all parties to a social agreement that it should be reached and perennial debilitating conflict reduced, or at least ordered in legally conventional ways. But the various parties finding it necessary to reach an agreement are not equal, for example, some may be rich and powerful, others may be poor, needy and relatively powerless. Self interest, in this context as in all others, is backed by greater or lesser power; and law, when it is promulgated, will reflect this. However, in many instances the interests of the powerful may be modified because excessive appropriation may indirectly threaten 'the power to do wrong' and thus a sort of balance is achieved through, as Barry points out, 'a bargaining solution'.[27] Ensuing law does not guarantee equality because the demands of the powerful will, so far as possible, be enshrined in its framing, at best it safeguards the weak from the greater depredations of the powerful. What will have been achieved is a situation in which matters for all the principal parties concerned are in no worse a condition, and possibly a little better, than if they had not agreed.[28] Barry remarks that in 'this theory of justice ... no special motive for behaving justly has to be invoked. Justice is simply rational prudence ... where the co-operation ... of other people is a condition of our being able to get what we want.'[29] Nietzsche adopted a similar position, but employed it differently.[30] Barry's arguments for rejecting this theory need not concern us here.

Barry's second theory removes the dependence on simple self-interest as a basis for the formulation of law and justice by rejecting the position in which power gives the upper hand to specific parties in this notional bargaining. He does this by introducing the moral concepts of impartiality and fairness, accompanied by a shift from the entirely solipsistic arguments of the self-interested, in favour of maximising their personal or corporate advantage, to arguments which will serve everyone.[31] This works by starting from the assumption that self-interested acquisitiveness resolves itself into something like the proposition 'Because I want x and have the power to take it, I have a right to x', which entails the authority of similar propositions from all other contenders for x. Barry suggests that the motivation for shifting from this 'realist' amoral position to moral judgement arises because, quoting Adam Smith: 'The man within immediately calls to us, that we value ourselves too much and other people too little, and that, by doing so, we render ourselves the proper object of the contempt and indignation of our brethren.'[32] However it may be worked out in detail there is, in Barry's view, a sort of loose moral consensus about what is right and what is wrong throughout humanity and it is to this that Adam Smith is appealing. Barry expresses it as a need for justification which, of course, elides into a need for justice. While it might be urged that the position could be subsumed under the 'realist' argument, that not to be held in contempt, to be justified, is an 'x' which 'I' want, it can immediately be seen that the proposition is self-defeating. Nonetheless, there is nothing in logic, as Barry points out, that compels the acceptance of moral precept as a foundation for justice, he merely observes that it is 'persuasive'. But what it persuades us to is the recognition that achievement of our own ends is commonly enhanced by taking into account, that is recruiting or being recruited by, those of other people. This may properly be described as 'impartiality' or 'fairness', the moral precept to be observed in the creation of law and regulation.[33] Nietzsche began from a curious mix of both positions, but notably employed them to restate Glaucon's position. In his account:

> Justice at the earliest stage of its development is the good will which prevails among those of roughly equal power to come to terms with one another, to 'come to an understanding' once more through a settlement – and to *force* those who are less powerful to agree a settlement among themselves.[34]

Barry's second theory seems to circumvent the major problem, often to be found in the related discourses of human rights, which is that of ascertaining the ground for ethical precepts. It is well illustrated in that standard work, *Human Rights in the World*. Its authors, A.H. Robertson and J.G. Merrills, arguing for the universality of human rights, point to the gradual change from a late-nineteenth-century nation state point of view, that international law may only regulate relations between states and may not protect the rights of individuals within nations, to the increasing recognition that 'the fundamental rights of the individual are a matter of international law, with international remedies available if those standards are not respected'.[35] We may feel that the change is gradual indeed: many powerful social-democrat states, let alone more authoritarian governments, are fighting very hard against that tide, but the change is apparent and the laws and institutions of international justice protecting the rights of individuals are slowly being created. Human rights theorists tend to turn for their inspiration to those bodies of law and those constitutions which explicitly embody the concept, in particular the Constitutions of Revolutionary France and the USA together with their subsequent elaborations in law. Robertson and Merrill, in their somewhat sketchy introduction to differing cultural accounts of human rights, begin with 'The liberal tradition of the Western democracies'.[36] We may treat their sweeping remark that the concept of human rights originates in European liberal democracy which, in turn, springs from 'Greek philosophy, Roman law, the Judaeo-Christian tradition, the humanism of the Reformation and the Age of Reason' with a decent reserve: they are neither historians nor philosophers. But they are forceful in their assertion that the primary formulations of the validity of human rights are to be found in the adoption by the National Assembly of France, on 26 August 1789, of the Declaration of the Rights of Man and the Citizen and in the Declaration of Rights uttered by the North American Continental Congress on 14 October 1774, just under two years prior to the Declaration of Independence and the emergence of the USA.

The problem with these two formulations lies in their justifications. Chief among the influences on the French Declaration are Montesquieu's[37] monumental *The Spirit of the Law* and the philosophical writings of Jean-Jaques Rousseau, particularly *The Social Contract* and *A Discourse on the Origin of Inequality*. Neither author was much concerned with the question raised by Barry about the foundation of justice and both regarded it, more or less, as self-evident. Rousseau is probably the most cavalier of the two, but caustically remarks: 'All justice comes from God, who is its sole source; but if we knew how to receive so high an inspiration, we should need neither government nor laws.'[38] By recasting the old proverb so that 'God proposes, but man disposes' Rousseau has effectively evaded the central questions of the basis of justice. In the next paragraph he dismisses what he calls 'attaching purely metaphysical ideas to the word [law]', and so elides the words 'justice' and 'law' and offers the 'general will' of the whole people as the only legitimate source of law-giving. We may well agree with him, but then everything depends on the ways in which the general will is established, how and by what means it is interpreted; Rousseau's responses to these questions are not our direct concern in this book. He enunciates Glaucon's position in an elegant sentence, 'In the state of nature, where everything is common, I owe nothing to him whom I have promised nothing; I recognise as belonging to others only what is of no use to me', but simply asserts that '[i]n the state of society all rights are fixed by law' – states of nature and of society are so radically different in his analysis that, for him, no further comment is necessary.[39] The North American Declaration and its descendants owe a great deal to elements in English law, and much of the rebellion by its proponents was against the refusal of the English ruling classes to administer that law equitably. Robertson and Merrills identify the *Magna Carta*, *Habeas Corpus* and the Bill of Rights of 1689 as among the principal English influences, but we may observe that all of them were concessions wrenched from the Crown by other ruling interests. English law has always been founded on Barry's first theory – the triumph of the will of the strongest enshrined in the very structure of adversarial justice. Thomas Jefferson, of course, determined the issue of the theory of justice by unequivocally deriving the legitimacy of the people from 'the Laws of Nature and of Nature's God' which resulted in the celebrated, but ultimately oxymoronic sentence: 'We hold these truths to be self-evident, that all men are created equal, that they are endowed by their Creator with certain unalienable rights, that among these are life, liberty and the pursuit of happiness.' The contradiction arises because, when they are understood as theophanic gifts, equality and liberty are dubious concepts. Collectively, these formulations make up a messy foundation for theories of human rights or justice.

Messiness in itself is not a difficulty, but the overall problem is set out succinctly by Harvey: he remarks that '[t]o argue for a particular definition of social justice has always implied ... appeal to some higher order criteria to define which theory ... is more just than another'.[40] Aeschylus, in his account of the trial of Orestes, met the challenge of competing social imperatives (theories) by putting the question to a jury of citizens established on Mount Areopagus by Pallas Athene. But the casting vote, in the case of an even division, was reserved to her, the all-wise 'higher order'.[41] Barry together with Rawls, on whose work he is building, both seem to be influenced heavily by Kant's view of the necessity of mutual respect for autonomous rational wills. This is the fount of the move from the first to the second of Barry's theories because Kant maintained that it was the possession of autonomous will which defined a person. The Kantian will generates principles, but they are only right and truly moral if they are capable of becoming universal.[42] So far as it goes, we may see in this a legitimisation of an appeal to 'some higher order criteria' since although the 'order' in this case is to be found in the same place as the appeal, the human community, it takes some form of hierarchical priority in Kant's account of the generation of principles. He effectively constructs a foundation for justice by the aggregation of those principles and starts from a definition of the individual – which, of course, is roughly where all idealist philosophers begin. But his position is novel in the progress of idealist philosophy since he maintains that it is the autonomous will which generates principles and so defines the person. Kant notoriously justified this argument by resorting to an astonishingly teleological account of the will which derived from what he called his Copernican revolution in philosophy,[43] in which objects take the forms they do because of the ways in which we know them. It would not be entirely misguided to see, in Kant's revolution, the origins of that extreme cultural relativism expressed by Lyotard despite the latter's dismissal of Kantian philosophy as collapsed 'metanarrative'.[44] Our objections to idealism are set out in Chapter 2 and have lain behind all our subsequent criticism, but we may add to them a rejection of teleological justification or explanation. Here, we may introduce a new difficulty: principles thus generated can only become universal by common consent: who, then, assembles these principles and by what means? We must also ask how the authority to judge universality is vested. Barry seems to be aware of the difficulty in his suggestion of a more or less universal loose moral consensus.

Harvey offers an example, not exactly of such a consensus, but of the socio-geographical formation of our sense of what is just. It is to do with retributive justice and is taken from a novel by Tony Hillerman;[45] he offers the suggestion that the 'landscape', that is, the complex of influences – societal, historical and familial – which shape our perceptions, 'functions as a mnemonic, alive with particular meanings, upon which native-Americans typically hang their sense of collective identity and values ... [which] speaks for a certain notion of justice'. This is, of course, an elegant version of one of the linguistic strands that we have discussed in Chapter 2. Harvey suggests that there are two principal ways of proceeding with the argument. One is to consider 'how the multiple concepts of justice are embedded in language' which, he observes, would lead on to theories like Wittgenstein's families of meanings, in which meanings may not be universally identical, but are, nonetheless, interrelated. The second is to 'interpret social justice as embedded in the hegemonic discourses of any ruling class or ruling faction', a position taken, in their very different ways, by Nietzsche and Marx and Engels. Harvey's two lines of argument make clear that he is not confining his discussion only to one form of justice and makes the point that Engels recognised that despite the hegemonic social conditioning of the meaning of justice imposed by a ruling class, it was, nonetheless, 'a powerful mobilising discourse for political action (as, for example, in the French Revolution)'. To this we would add the obvious point that Harvey's two lines of argument are not mutually exclusive, but closely linked.

For practitioners and theorists of development operating within the institutions – educational, governmental or non-governmental – of the industrialised world, the issue of socially just and, therefore, sustainable development is a minefield. Discussions of sustainability, either in environmental or economic terms, are less nakedly confrontational. To a considerable degree both are to do with second order perceptions; that is to say, that no matter how degraded a given environment may become as a consequence of human activity, or how poor people may be rendered by larger economic movement, it commonly takes a more or less sophisticated argument to establish the necessary links between circumstance and cause. Justice, in all its meanings, running from the concept of fairness to much of the complexity of law-giving, impinges directly on the consciousness of everyone subject to law. Unfairness in distributive justice is an everyday experience for the world's poor. It is, for example, driven home even more sharply in the countless cases of the dispossession of peasant farmers in favour of industrial farming and the eviction of 'illegal' squatters around many of the world's major cities.[46] Recognition of injustice at the hands of ruling classes is, in these circumstances, immediate. Neither peasants nor squatters (among many others) are foolish enough not to see that their persecution at the hands of the law-givers is supported by, in some way derives from, the even more powerful law-givers of the industrialised world. Their response to agendas promoting social justice from international institutions of development may, in consequence, be similar to that of the Trojans to Greeks bearing gifts.[47]

Over a decade ago, Ben Wisner wrote a lively book, based on his extensive and committed work in Africa, defending what he called a 'strong Basic Needs Approach (BNA)'. In his introduction he remarked:

> Criticism of efforts to stem the deterioration of the human environment in the Third World has come from the Left and the Right. The Left says that the programmes were cosmetic and never addressed the underlying economic forces that drive poor people to expand their farms into forested lands, to over graze pastures, to cut trees for sale of charcoal or to squat in unsanitary slums near dangerous factories. The Right has revived a Malthusian interpretation ... environmental programmes are bound to fail if they do not face up to the challenge of unchecked population growth.[48]

The present authors are, of course, part of that left and our response would be to say that whatever proposals may be made for the alleviation of catastrophic problems, not to understand and, where necessary, to attack the underlying causes of the devastation of people's lives and environments may well be to collaborate in the onslaught. But beneath the slightly lazy debating point (between left and right – the extremes – sensible people will find a middle ground), Wisner's BNA is likely to be both effective and politically productive. It calls for the recognition that people in need are perfectly capable of determining what they need for themselves and, given the space, are probably better at organising resources than any expert sent to do it for them.

In describing forms of basic need, Wisner is, in terms of our discussion, pointing to the failure, the absence, of equitable distributive justice. He offers a model table for indicating that basic needs are not being met;[49] the value of such tables is that they remind us of the reality that we are addressing and we have adapted Wisner's model to illustrate degrees of injustice (table 5.1). In it we have compared statistics from one of Sub-Saharan Africa's poorest countries (Uganda) and an only marginally less destitute South Asian state (Nepal) with similar figures, where they are available, from Britain. Disparities like these are appallingly familiar and it is worth noting that even in those indicators where some improvement is shown, it is small and painfully slow. Life expectancy in Uganda actually declined in the twenty-seven years covered by the figures.

Table 5.1   Indicators of Comparative Basic Needs (Uganda, Nepal, UK)

Indicator	Uganda		Nepal		UK	
Life expectancy (years)	1970	1997	1970	1997	1970	1997
	46	41	42	57	72	77
Infant mortality (per 1000 live births)	1980	1996	1980	1996	1980	1996
	116	99	132	85	12	6
Primary school attendance (%)	male	female	male	female	male	female
	65	63	80	60	100	100
Secondary school attendance (%)	male	female	male	female	male	female
	15	9	49	25	100	100
	1990–97		1990–97		1990–97	
Underweight under 5s (%)	26		47		n/a*	
Wasting under 5s (%)	5		11		n/a	
Stunting under 5s (%)	38		48		n/a	

*See note 50
Sources: UNDP, 1998; World Bank, 1998/99; UNICEF, 1999.

Distributive justice, like all other forms of justice, is normative and because its function is to determine what goods that people (individuals, groups, societies, classes, perhaps nations) are to enjoy, it must operate, or be constructed, according to particular precepts. This is true whether we think of incomes and opportunities or of services and goods like shelter, health, education and consumables. We may have no difficulty in seeing the disparities illustrated in table 5.1 as unjust, but agreement on what precepts are to inform distributive justice are commonly ground for dispute. For example, our table typifies an extensive range of worldwide inequalities and to reduce them would seem to argue for the precept of equality. Norms are relatively inflexible since they are the standards around which law is formed, thus a definition of equality, if it is to be used as a principle of distributive justice, would seem to be called for. Transfers of resources from rich countries or people to the poor may, it has often been observed, give benefits to the poor greater than any harm it may do to the living standards of the rich.[51] Mechanisms could undoubtedly be devised to allow for such transfers, but while some suffering might be alleviated it will do little to diminish disparities or to promote equality. If egalitarianism is to inform distributive justice, then it becomes necessary to recognise what must be considered. Could it, for instance, embrace equality in economic and political power, or should it refer only to equality of opportunity to secure 'adequate' access to social and economic goods? If the former, how is this to be achieved where both are so heavily concentrated in such a small number of states, institutions and people? If the latter, how probable does it seem in the face of rampant capital–capital competition and capital–labour exploitation? Other similarly contentious areas must also enter the discussion – resources, welfare and freedom are among them.

Philosophers of law, like other specialising philosophers, tend to exclude other considerations from their analyses; we may recall Wittgenstein's caustic aphorism: 'The philosopher's treatment of a question is like the treatment of an illness.'[52] One result of this is the development of hermeneutics which, no matter how thoroughly distinctions are made, leave the interested observer wondering how it is possible to attach them to reality. We may see this readily in philosophical discussions of distributive justice summarised in the *Stanford Encyclopaedia of Philosophy*.[53] In the entry headed 'Justice, Distributive' its author distinguishes no fewer than six groups of more or less exclusive principles on which such justice may be built or analysed. Of these, 'strict egalitarianism', in which everyone should enjoy all goods and services equally, is the first. Next is the 'difference principle' which, as the author points out, was advocated by Rawls who first elaborated it in a paper given in 1958[54] and then developed it in his later work; it was an idea to which he continuously returned and which was subsequently developed by Barry.[55] In the difference principle, the personal right to 'basic liberties' is governed by its compatibility with a 'system of liberty for all'; economic and social disparities must be addressed in ways which will allow for 'the benefit of the least advantaged' and where those disparities are caused by differing rewards for employment, then those jobs must be offered on the basis of equal and fair opportunity. The third distinction covers 'resource-based principles' in which no one should be penalised because of circumstances beyond their control; while access to goods and services may well be conditioned by a person's life choices, anyone handicapped by accident of birth should be especially supported. 'Welfare-based principles' form the fourth category, they flow from the assumption that, in any given society, it is morally repugnant to allow people to fall below a certain generally acceptable level of welfare. Fifth in this catalogue come 'desert-based principles': beloved of Margaret Thatcher, these comprise roughly three versions of 'you get what you deserve', you are rewarded for the value of what you contribute to society, or for how hard you work, or to cover your costs in working. Finally, the author lists 'libertarian principles' which differ radically from the previous five: they are governed by the view that certain 'acquisitions or exchanges … are themselves just'; these may or may not be market transactions since justice does not, in the libertarian view, depend on any single mode of exchange, but on a standard engendered by the justice of separate transactions between individuals.

There is, of course, a fundamental contradiction between capitalist accumulation and its consequent competition and exploitation on the one hand, and any account of an equal society on the other. Competition is dependent on differentials or, in any circumstance in which competitors are equal, is dependent on the creation of at least a measure of inequality – one party or another is normally expected to win. Even supposing that the competing parties are more or less evenly matched, it is an inherently unstable system. Indirectly, Rawls remarks on that instability in a paragraph about the role of the state in another early paper (1967) entitled 'Distributive Justice'.[56] We have repeatedly pointed to the extent to which capitalism depends for its ideological justification on philosophical enquiries which begin with the individual and with individual competition. That such reasoning is widely accepted throughout the industrialised world constitutes the most extraordinary sleight of hand on the part of its establishments, demonstrated by the cant about 'level-playing fields' in world trade and the 'tyranny' of labour combination in response to the demands of corporations. None of the six distinctions of the principles of distributive justice, as outlined in the *Stanford Encyclopaedia*, challenges individualistic transactions as a basis for formulating the principles of some socially just distribution, not even the last of them which seems dimly to appreciate that the market cannot safely be left as the final arbiter of anything. Nonetheless, three of these distinctions, based on a morality emerging from a modified Kantianism, dominate the contemporary debate about justice; they are the difference, the resource-based and the welfare-based principles. Just as Socrates recognised Glaucon's position as the most serious threat to his own view, we, in a manner less likely to influence the progress of the world, must briefly examine these three in order to offer criticism.

In the industrialised world, debate about distributive justice is dominated by the work of John Rawls. He offered his 'original position' as part of a major refutation of the utilitarianism of R.B. Braithwaite who, in his inaugural lecture in 1955 for the Chair of Moral Philosophy in the University of Cambridge, had responded to a problem posed by the mathematician J.F. Nash, known as the 'Bargaining Problem', which is important in this discussion because of the concept we have been examining that justice and law are the product of some sort of social bargain. He reformulated the problem by assuming two musicians, Matthew, a trumpeter and Luke, a pianist who worked in adjacent and by no means sound-proof rooms; these two had only the same hour in each day in which to practice and both of them found it difficult to do so while the other was playing. The problem begins with the question of how the available time could most fairly be divided between them, the solution depends on finding what is known as the point of 'Pareto optimality'.[57] If the musicians fail to agree on any division of the time, then clearly neither benefits, therefore any agreement is better than not to agree at all. However, to move from non-agreement to Pareto optimality demands that the point of non-agreement must be established which may, in some process of arbitration, be arrived at by discovering any points of partial agreement. On a scale of one to six, where six is the point of Pareto optimality, let us suppose that the musicians, having settled the first three points are searching for ways to settle the second three to the greatest advantage of each. The two musicians have agreed on certain utilities and the arbitrator, in Braithwaite's account, may now help them to move forward.

Braithwaite pointed out, in his lecture, that there was no automatic or established point of non-agreement between the two musicians and that each, in reaching that point, would do his utmost to secure the greatest advantage for himself before the Pareto optimal is applied. But these relative advantages need not be the same for each of the parties. Both of them would prefer to play without competition from the other and they would both rather not play while the other is practising. But Matthew's choice for his second preference would be that both musicians should play because silence is of less importance to him as a trumpeter. Luke, on the other hand, would prefer silence to discord. These differences allow each contestant to apply different 'threats' in the process of arbitration and they will do so in order to achieve the greatest possible advantage to themselves; 'advantage', as we have pointed out, must also include preferences. Since the pianist, Luke, prefers silence, he is in the weaker position because if he does not play in order to achieve it he allows Matthew unopposed enjoyment of his first preference. Matthew wields the greater threat and hence, in any process of bargaining, would gain the greater amount of uncontested playing time (his first preference); this could be virtually any amount less than 100 per cent consonant with Luke's acceptance, no matter how grudging, of the deal. Enough would have to be given to Luke commensurate with the strength of his desire for silence while playing which is his only preference. Here Braithwaite objects, because any solution heavily weighted in Matthew's favour would manifestly be unfair, though he says that he would not expect the musicians to accept an agreement simply based on fairness.

Neither the remainder of this argument, nor the solution suggested by Braithwaite, need concern us here, its importance for us lies in its place as the springboard for Rawls's development of it.[58] Nash and Braithwaite are both, in their different ways, examining Glaucon's position and, like Rawls and Barry, are unhappy with the Socratic solution. Braithwaite's doubtful appeal to 'fairness' is really to 'some higher order criteria'; Rawls, positing his 'original position' offers a justification for that appeal. Arbiters, including the one between Matthew and Luke, are asked to adopt a 'veil of ignorance', which the *Stanford Encyclopaedia* describes as a central part of 'a methodological device for ridding the ethico-political "observer" of hindrances to h/er clear and distinct perception of ethico-political facts'.[59] These hindrances are the sum of our social characteristics, our race, class, education, occupation, social position, wealth, beliefs and so on; the arbitrator's 'veil of ignorance' consists of setting knowledge of these aside in order to make the best choice of the principles of public morality since, acting in ignorance of her or his own social condition, the arbitrator will naturally choose what is best for everyone. D'Agostino remarks that the practical consequences of this approach do not seem 'to have been adequately conceptualised',[60] a comment that the present writers would endorse.

In proposing his 'original position' Rawls seems to us to have weakened the whole concept of the social contract as a product of the bargaining solution. We feel this to be no bad thing since 'social contract' and 'bargaining' are epistemic terms, embodying specific and unanalysed values, which pre-empt much of the argument. Rawls's proposal shifts the focus of the argument about the principles of distributive justice away from bargaining for mutual advantage towards achieving justice through impartiality,[61] but it does not, because that is not its business, help us to define the arena in which 'impartiality' is to operate. Bargaining to establish a body of justice was for, among others, Plato, Nash and Braithwaite, a system of ever-widening concentric circles at the centre of which stand the parties to the bargain. Eventually these circles (areas of agreement) meet similar circles from elsewhere with similar centres and bargaining (or war) begins between them. By this means local agreement progresses to civic, national and international law and, in such a system, what constitutes social contract arises from perpetual accommodation to *force majeure*. The very word 'contract' incorporates the idea of bargain; thus the *OED*: 'A mutual agreement between two or more parties that something shall be done or forborne by one or both; a compact, covenant, bargain; especially such as has legal effects.' In advocating a blind impartiality Rawls sufficiently subverts the structure of contract or bargain to make them, in the context, difficult to use. There is, too, an obvious difficulty in understanding how the final agreement is to be made to adopt, as a body of law, a bundle of impartial judgements about what is most beneficial for all. The argument becomes circular if that decision is also to be reached by a rule of impartiality.

We may recognise the Rawls–Barry endeavour as an heroic attempt at civilising the process of capitalist law-making without disturbing the foundations on which it is built. There are plausible reasons for making such efforts; some amelioration of the lot of the vulnerable might be achieved and that would be better than nothing; reform may stand a better chance than revolution. Gradualism, of the kind advocated for so long by the Second International, may in this view bring us more rapidly to the revolutionary target. Its adherents see, for example, the Blairite marriage of international corporate capital and social management as an historical accident, a hiccough in an otherwise continuous process. Evidence in support of this blithe optimism is hard to discover, evidence against it is thick on the ground and one simple example of the latter may be seen in the 'banana wars' between the USA and Europe. Glaucon's argument has bedevilled the formation and philosophy of law, at least in its more progressive moments, ever since it was first advanced. Distributive justice, like all other forms of legal arrangement, is about the sharing of resources and is always subject to the balance of powers. We have repeatedly made the point that no matter how potentially powerful popular opposition may be, organised power remains in the hands of the TNC giants and of their enabling wealthy states. In principle, little has changed since Marx and Engels made the point in 1872:

> The lower strata of the middle class – the small trades-people, shopkeepers … the handicraftsmen and peasants – all these sink gradually into the proletariat, partly because their diminutive capital does not suffice for the scale on which Modern Industry is carried on, and is swamped in the competition with the large

capitalists, partly because their specialised skill is rendered worthless by new methods of production.

> The modern labourer ... instead of rising with the progress of industry, sinks deeper and deeper below the conditions of existence of his own class. He becomes a pauper, and pauperism develops more rapidly than population and wealth.[62]

Marx and Engels were writing and campaigning within the industrialised world of their time, but their comments may be applied, just as aptly, to the globe as a whole. No one remains unaffected by contemporary capital and its economic arrangements.

We have argued that development is unsustainable unless it is socially just. We have also argued that because contemporary capital is inherently socially destructive, social justice cannot be expected under its sway. Much distributive law, indeed much law, is now regulated, administered and formulated by international institutions given, like the WTO, legal personality and the power to override national laws and social agreements where they are judged to impede free trade. During the protest at the WTO's Third Ministerial Conference in Seattle against the extension of that bureaucracy's powers, the fact that the powerful member states were compelling weaker members to dismantle their protective instruments while, at the same time, refusing to move on their own became a matter of public debate. One of the more notorious agreements constructed in the course of the campaign for free trade, and subsumed under the mantle of the WTO, is the NAFTA. Mexico is the United States' third largest trading partner (Japan and Canada are the other two) and the US absorbs 70 per cent of its exports. Without its giant neighbour, Mexico's economy would collapse; it almost did in 1995, when, under Clinton's administration, the US bailed it out to the tune of US$48 billion. That economic crisis hugely increased unemployment, drove countless small farmers into destitution and depressed yet further already chronically low industrial wages. Among its causes was the implementation of the NAFTA. Over 2 million workers were put out of work because Mexican manufacture was unable to compete with the cheap goods dumped on its market by the US under the free trade terms of the Agreement.[63] Numbers of US TNCs, or their surrogates, took advantage of this huge pool of cheap labour and the absence of any environmental regulation and set up the *maqiladora* industries, particularly along the border. For many workers in the US it meant chronic unemployment; for the exploited and unprotected workers of Mexico, even the pittances offered under this arrangement were an improvement on the unemployment by then rampant in the country.[64] In addition to these calamities, Mexico, prior to the agreement, was already home to some of the most polluting industries in the world, but the substantial movement into the country of US industry increased the problem exponentially: 'More than 1,000 *maqiladoras* were set up in Mexico after NAFTA went into effect.'[65] Environmental problems are serious, but, since they also affect the border regions of the US, some effort is at last being made to deal with them; wages, on the other hand, have not improved since 1994 'when the hourly wage differential between the United States and Mexico reached a whopping 12 to 1'.[66] Simultaneously with the creation of these underpaid jobs, the Agreement also prevents the Mexican state from interfering with the ownership and practices of the TNCs and forbids it to introduce performance standards. The latter is important because minimal standards might compel TNCs to introduce technology to Mexico which would allow indigenous enterprises to compete.[67] Mexico's development as an unregulated, kind of poor-law workhouse for US capital is unsustainable on many grounds; we offer it here simply as an example, by no means unique, of law and, hence, justice derived from capital.

One consequence of our view of capitalist justice is that the very concept of socially just development is called into question, since contemporary justice is founded on *force majeure* and not on some principle of equity or fairness. Hence, it seems to us, Glaucon's position is unassailable, but it is also commonly misunderstood. That concepts of justice evolve within the societies in which they are held is a truism, but their evolution is consequent on a complex of interests and powers whose proponents are all fighting for their position. The Pareto optimal is achieved when those of greater power have settled things sufficiently to their advantage without so compromising the position of the weaker that social stability is threatened. Idealist ways of thinking, in which the world is primarily one of individualised consciousness, leave only, as in the case of Rawls, an appeal to 'fairness' as a means of modifying the demands of the powerful. The inadequacy of such an appeal is amply demonstrated by, on the one hand, the despotism of a Saddam Hussein or, on the other, the rank opportunism of Thatcherite 'New' Labour. Barry is obviously aware of this, hence his attempt at constructing new argument designed to rescue Rawls from his dilemma.

If, however, the argument is moved away from individuals to society, the need to defeat Glaucon's proposition recedes. Justice becomes a matter of *class*, not analysable on the model of individual bargaining. Despite Hegel's classic analysis of class as fixed, presumably forever, by the natural order of things, modern conservatives of all parties, or none, have always attempted to defuse Marxist analysis by identifying class, not in terms of the relationship to the means of production, but of social habit. With the demise of much manufacturing in the older industrialised states, this has enabled them to postulate the extinction of the working class because they have insisted on the capitalist *mores* of a particular period as its defining circumstances. That persistent absurdity was effectively attacked by Marx himself,[68] but, nonetheless, it survives among its proponents as a useful piece of propaganda. Since advanced capitalism has globalised its activities, has industrialised agrarian production and has expanded its control, so the working class has grown immensely beyond the confines of the nineteenth-century industrial world. It incorporates the dispossessed, the poor throughout the world who have been thrust to the margins of productive existence or pushed into modern industrial agricultural production for the international market; it includes the exploited workers in contemporary sweatshops; above all, its ranks are rapidly and enormously increased by the proletarianisation of displaced peasants.[69] Many of the forms of work have changed and there is a growing army of white-collar proletarians in, for example, the industries based on telecommunications and computer technology.

It has not been uncommon, even among socialists, to think of justice in the abstract; that is to suppose that there is some standard by which it might be measured – such a perception may also lie behind Rawls' appeal to fairness. From a class perspective justice and law do not depend either on an abstraction or on any 'higher order criterion', but on the ability of the class concerned to identify its common needs and to enforce their recognition. Social justice is a battleground in class struggle in which, so far, a ludicrously unstable ruling capitalist class has been the victor. Twentieth-century

Communism failed not merely because of the power of global capital, but because it did not understand that 'democratic rights alone provide socialism with the political air it needs to breathe'.[70] Twenty-first century capital, whose primary product is further capital produced by the extraction of yet more and more surplus value from a smaller and smaller working force,[71] may fail not only because of the strength of the vastly increased working class, but because it does not recognise that people, either as producers or as consumers, are an essential ingredient in their escalation of profit. The reasons for the working-class fight for its own justice have not really changed, but the scale of the fight is immeasurably greater and many of its forms are other. Chief among those changes is the location of the struggle; once it was within the factory, the point of physical production, now it must extend to that amorphous region of the production of finance capital.

We are contending that Glaucon was fundamentally right, and that objections arise only because contemporary interpretations have insisted on, as a model for understanding, a notional social contract between individuals. What counts as justice is determined by power – as we have already remarked, Nietzsche, with a different agenda, made a similar point. It is always necessary, therefore, not only to examine the foundations of the law under which we demand social justice, but the degree to which it is compromised by the power relations of the society which has produced it. Recent events in international trade such as genetic patenting, increased US and EU protectionism against struggling economies, massively increased dumping and so on are commonly in accordance with capitalist laws. This presents many of the larger international non-governmental development organisations with a particular difficulty, because in seeking to integrate poorer communities into the basic benefits of social democracy, they must appeal for justice against the laws of their own social-democratic states. Not to do so is to collude in the absurdity of supposing that the world's poor can be introduced to the affluence of the contemporary middle classes.

That dilemma is illustrated in the introductory chapters to the first volume of *The Oxfam Handbook of Development and Relief*,[72] which is one of the most enlightened and unexceptionable of NGO statements of intent. Its authors remark that 'people's capacity to determine their own values and priorities, and to organise ... and to act ... is the basis of development'; that people and their needs must be at the centre of all development and relief; that they must be empowered to take control of their own lives and to bring about necessary change. Issues connected with race and gender will, if not properly addressed, actually disempower people; full participation in all projects and programmes is essential. The concept of sustainability is sensibly modified to allow for work which may be rendered unsustainable by circumstances beyond the control of the people concerned. Above all, social justice must be achieved and human rights protected. It is to the authors' credit that they extend these understandings to relief as well as to development.

What is missing from this admirable scheme of things is a careful definition of terms. Social justice, for example, is simultaneously an abstract concept and, in its particularities, a practical, quotidian set of laws and regulations. Even when the latter offer a modicum of protection, they may extensively be modified by *force majeure*, but, most importantly, we are back precisely to the issues raised in this chapter. Exactly whose justice are we addressing? It may be the case that INGOs can only deal with the issue by trying to right particular wrongs and their members may feel either that there is nothing substantially wrong with existing social-democratic law, or that it is beyond their remit to address such wrongs if they do actually see them. This criticism applies right across the board: while there may be room, particularly in relatively limited projects, simply to help matters along a little without troubling too much about longer term questions, the language of Oxfam's *Handbook* is universalist in tone. In dealing with GATT and the WTO, the authors quite rightly attack the grosser abuses in the programmes of those organisations – particularly the threat of dismantling much national social and environmental protection in the interests of free trade. What they do not consider is the entirely possible circumstance in which these extravagances may be overcome, by suitable regulatory modification, without touching the central, competitive and humanly destructive process of TNC capital accumulation. It is obviously our contention that justice and law are not neutral in any of their aspects. For example, in Brazil, despite the undoubtedly courageous resistance to the state's fiscal and agricultural policies by landless peasants in general and women's movements in particular, by the beginning of the 1990s there were between 10 million and 20 million landless people who had been driven from their land by the rapid growth of industrialised agriculture. But among even those smallholders who had survived, as, for instance, in the state of Rio Grande do Sul, huge numbers were involved in land conflicts. The state capital was anxious to keep the smallholder sector going because it was heavily dependent on it for the production of food for the towns and raw materials for industrial agriculture, yet it continued its legal war of attrition in favour of the agricultural corporations.[73]

We scarcely need such examples. For generations TNCs have taken over or crushed independent and alternative modes of production, in the interest of greater and greater control of productive chains and in the pursuit of profit. State, international and supranational bodies of law exist to facilitate the process. Unless this problem is understood and examined, sustainability begins, as a concept, to fray not merely at the edges, but at its centre. In the next chapter we shall look at some of the consequences of our systematic criticism of the ground on which much current discussion rests.

6
Everlasting Groans
(Milton, *Paradise Lost*, Bk.2, 184)

In the last three chapters we have argued that no unalloyed account can be given of the three main categories in which sustainability in development and relief is normally judged. The concept is always conditioned by the complex of presuppositions – environmental, economic and jurisprudential – with which its users invest it. What we think about environmental sustainability is profoundly affected by our view not just of nature, but of the relationship of humanity to it. It is modified, too, by our difficulty in recognising ourselves in what Marx called our 'species being'. Above all, capital has taught us to see the environment as so much property, a view which alienates us further from the reality of our part in it. Economic sustainability is even more clearly a matter for political choice; those working in development and humanitarian assistance are largely compelled to accept the political choices of those providing the funds and of the states in which they work. Decisions are made about projects and programmes on the basis of whether or not they will survive the period in which funds are available, or whether or not they will survive in the economic climate in which they will subsequently have to operate. Little attention is ever given to the macro-economic ends to which livelihoods might be directed. In many ways, judgements about economic sustainability are extremes in short-termism. Social justice, as a condition for sustainability, is the most serious area of contention; the liberal (in its generous sense) analysis is hopelessly entangled in the fruitlessness of trying to escape Glaucon's question rather than accepting it and dealing with it. Its one redeeming feature is that it compels us to ask whose social justice is at issue and in which society is it exercised.

Running through these difficulties is the even more complex issue not only of how we use language, but, even more importantly, how we think it works. We began our argument by setting out our account of the way language is used because it is no longer possible to consider major social, political and ideological questions without declaring a linguistically political starting point. It is our view that the determinism of the post-modernist analysis of language (to be distinguished clearly from any Wittgensteinian linguistic analysis) springs from a profoundly capitalist philosophy – it is, so to say, the final idealist ideological justification of neo-liberalism in which Lyotard, a Kantian, can attack Kant. Beckett chronicled the disaster: Krapp is silent as he listens to his last tape and Mouth, in *Not I*, is no longer a person.[1] It has become necessary to understand the hegemony of capital, which has taught us to think in its terms; we have not only to reconstruct relations of property and production, gender and society, but also, in a sense, the roots of consciousness.

All this terrain is difficult, but not impossible, in a relatively small way it is even familiar. Dealing with conscious, semi-conscious and unconscious racism is a common experience, particularly in industrialised countries. The politically essential process for which we are arguing is very similar to, even, to a considerable degree, inclusive of, that continuing battle. Reconstructing our consciousness is, however, a lengthy project and one which can only grow organically out of the actual politics in which we are engaged. We have criticised the broad positions which we take to inform much contemporary thinking about sustainable development and have ended by dismissing them politically. Like Belial, however, we do not relish the prospect of condemning ourselves 'to converse in everlasting groans'; what does not follow from our argument is any case for demanding that Western governments and their agencies (including INGOs) should stop providing aid for development and relief. To do nothing at all is, notoriously, to opt for the *status quo* and railing against some obviously good and important work because its foundations are ideologically impure is absurd – it would be to adopt a position similar to that so ably demolished, in 1920, by Lenin.[2] Even those latter-day knights in shining armour, egregiously crying that their only purpose is to save lives as their meddling makes political situations worse,[3] have a point. Assistance for those in dire straits as a result either of some immediate crisis or of chronic poverty is essential. But there is a balance to be struck between the good that intervening will do and the long-term economic, social and political damage it may cause. Programmes of development and of humanitarian assistance are littered with instances in which the last case of those to be helped was rendered worse than the first and there are many others in which the human cost 'for the greater good' is unacceptable.[4] Our purpose is to clarify the intellectual and political processes in which we, our governments and their associated corporations are engaged and so to throw light on our political choices.

In recent years, much soul-searching has been undertaken at least in the more responsible of the international NGOs, not least because of several disastrous interventions in Rwanda. A Code of Conduct in disaster relief has been agreed by many NGOs and the international humanitarian agencies that make up the Red Cross and Red Crescent family. Other initiatives of this kind in the field of disaster response are the Sphere Project[5] which is establishing standards for delivering all humanitarian assistance and the Active Learning Network on Accountability and Performance in Humanitarian Aid (ALNAP). It is important to note, particularly in the case of these last two, that standards can never be translated into entitlements for those affected by disaster, because no guarantee can be given for the level of supplies that donors are likely to finance. Ethical codes applicable to development work also exist; one example, adopted in 1997, has been produced by the South African National NGO Coalition (SANGOCO). The importance of these endeavours should not be underestimated; they insist, among other things, on full consultation of and participation with the communities for which the projects are to be designed and implemented, on the recognition of the condition and separate needs of women, on the need for cultural sensitivity and, most importantly, on the importance of the political context of any intervention. These initiatives are relatively recent and evidence for the difference that they make in the field, if any, has not yet emerged. But no development or humanitarian NGO can be unaware of their existence and it is entirely reasonable to suggest that their major effect will be to inhibit the naivety exhibited so widely in interventions prior to, and including, Rwanda. Their language and prescriptions must penetrate even the shiniest armour and the dullest intellect of an NGO white knight.

Because Oxfam is unquestionably among the industrialised world's leading NGOs and firmly advocates the new codes of practice, we must look again at what might be called a declaration of faith offered in their *Handbook*. A major constituent of it comes in a powerful passage early in volume I:

> The processes of social, economic, political and cultural change ... do not have a clear beginning, middle and end ... Development and relief programmes constitute at most a limited and transient intervention in these processes. They focus on certain aspects of people's lives, such as their need to have food and shelter, to make a living, to deal with illness, or to press for legal and civil rights ... human life is a changing set of discrete components. There are no firm boundaries between, for example, a woman's reproductive health and her need for decent housing, or economic independence; or between these and her husband's belonging to the neighbourhood social committee; or her daughter's participation in an adult literacy programme.[6]

While we might take issue with the idea of the transience of relief programmes, since many of them may last for decades, these remarks are unexceptionable. Eade and Williams go on to complain that many NGOs, perfectly content to accept Oxfam's view, nonetheless concentrate 'on the micro level of projects' to the exclusion of 'the wider economic and political context'. The authors' remedy for this is to urge a clearer understanding of the concept of 'empowerment' and, in making this suggestion, they point to the differences between the way that the World Bank might understand it and what it would mean either to 'a militant peasant farmer's union or a conventional development NGO' (it is unclear whether, or not, Oxfam includes itself in this last category). Eade and Williams make the point that cooperation in some relatively small, but locally important, enterprise can lead communities on to larger questions. They see the process as progressive, but not automatic; for a variety of reasons people may have internalised their oppression and feel that their situation is part of the natural order (this is particularly true of women suffering from male violence), or that the specific struggle in which the community engages may fail to address other problems in some of its sectors. Despite these caveats, they remark that:

> Empowerment, in the context of development work, is essentially concerned with analysing and addressing the dynamics of oppression. Confronting the ways in which people internalise their low social status, with a resulting lack of self-esteem, and assisting groups and individuals to come to believe that they have a legitimate part to play in the decisions which affect their lives, is the beginning of empowerment.[7]

It would be unreasonable either to attack Oxfam for what is, after all, one of the best of INGO manifestos, or the authors for working in such a compressed space – their remarks are part of a general introduction to the real business of the *Handbook*. Nonetheless, some of the problems with which we are concerned are neatly illustrated here.

We have already remarked (towards the end of Chapter 5) on the failure of the authors to define their terms and, in Chapter 1, we mentioned the acute spatial and temporal limits to empowerment thus conceived. Integral to our argument is the relationship between individual and society, concepts which remain crucially undistinguished in these passages and are, consequently, confused. Oppressive regimes maintain their power by fragmenting social groups which might be the basis of an opposition and by uniting individuals in the regime's cause either in some ideology of its own or by terror. The process is well described by Marx in his account of the destruction by Louis Bonaparte, in the course of 1849, of the bourgeois revolutionaries of France.[8] Eade and Williams have, in noting the effect of violence against women, touched on one of the first steps in resistance to oppression, which is to bring people thus fragmented and isolated to the recognition of their *common* plight and thus to a united front. Individually traumatised women, either prevented by male violence from understanding their situation as anything but the norm or, in some cultures, too ashamed to bring it to light, must first be given the tools to escape their isolation. Such a process is offered as a model for the socio-political emancipation of all people divided by whatever cause and is obviously a route which frequently must be taken. But a central point is missed here: oppression may take the form of violence against women, bonded labour (slavery), military and police terror, corruption, censorship, the disempowerment of the poor and a whole panoply of other horrors, but none of these forms is directly the object of oppression. Each of them, individually and collectively, is part of the machinery needed by the regime to maintain power and each is a tool in the destruction of social community, the biggest threat to totalitarianism. It may be necessary to work, as it were, therapeutically with individuals, but the object is to re-establish community as the fundamental unit of social interaction and, therefore, of politics. It would not be hyperbolic to say that the essential work is to re-establish the possibility of humanity, since it is our contention that meaning can only be given to individuality in terms of community, or because, in another discourse, the two concepts are interdependent.

Our argument is not simply a matter of splitting hairs. Developmental thinking based on the model of empowerment set out by Eade and Williams sees the operative political unit as the individual who combines with other individuals to achieve an end. These individuals may then, perhaps, go on to discover other, wider, goals and, in working for their accomplishment, act as exemplars to others similarly placed; Fowler,[9] who is by no means alone, takes this position and we offered our criticism of it in Chapter 1. There our argument was that a micro-solution to a macro-problem stood little chance of success, micro-solutions can only work for micro-problems. Obviously, micro-solutions are frequently successful in their own terms; a great deal of development and relief work does alleviate immediate suffering and does facilitate livelihoods and it would be wrong to suggest that it should be abandoned. 'Micro' can also be a misleading adjectival prefix, since it may refer not to the absolute size of any given project, which could be quite large in the numbers of people involved, but to its specific aims. We are more concerned here with an epistemological and, hence, a political difficulty. If the conceptual starting point is individuals who may combine into individual groups which may combine further, not *ad infinitum*, because such a progress must collapse for want of a collective vision, but on some undefined and aspirational scale, then the conceptual aim of oppression has been adopted. The balance of responsibility has been tilted away from society and towards the individual, a subtle variant of blaming the victim.

Because poverty and its accompanying repressions are social and not just individual ills, solutions as opposed to mere ameliorations must also be social. For INGOs, this is treacherous ground since virtually all of them, to a greater or lesser degree are, at best, reflections of the societies that gave birth to them and, at worst, agents of governments which are parties to the creation of that worldwide poverty. Many NGOs, and again Oxfam is a good example, press for a reformist agenda and have been consistent in working as what might be called a 'loyal opposition' – a role which became apparent in the widespread condemnation of the MAI mounted well before the debacle in Seattle. See, for example, Oxfam's position paper of April 1998 entitled *Update on Proposed MAI*, though it had made several other public statements before and since. Oxfam was not unique in this matter, many other INGOs took similar positions. Christian Aid published a policy paper on fair trade criticising the WTO; it was entitled *Fair Shares: Transnational Companies, the WTO and the World's Poorest Countries*. The Catholic Fund for Overseas Development (CAFOD), also, lodged its protest in its *Briefing on the WTO in Seattle*, and there were many others around the world.[10] None of them address the central contradictions inherent in globalised finance capital for which the MAI and even the WTO were designed, and to which we have drawn attention.

Interestingly, Christian Aid goes further in calling its position paper on trade *Fair Shares*; the very word 'shares' is profoundly suspect. It conjures up a sense that if only prices commensurate with the value of what is produced were paid to impoverished workers and producers in the developing world, then they could escape from their poverty. But the process is still extractive, since even if they were permitted under existing agreements to add a greater degree of value in what they produce (finished goods rather than materials, refining processes and so on), they would be doing so for the benefit of those TNCs controlling that 80 per cent of trade and, hence, for the benefit of finance capital. All trade with the industrialised world is compromised and the argument for constructing a fairer MAI or WTO misses the point that we have repeatedly made, that capital is essentially competitive and depends on a system of winners and losers. It is necessarily centripetal and controls not only investment and profits but, famously, seeks to control all sectors of production –

the scramble for patenting genes should give us the greatest pause for thought.

Not only is capitalism and its necessary obsession with free trade (necessary because regulation is understood as an impediment to the continuous increase of profit) trying totally to control all possible chains of production and consumption, it is also anxious to control our perceptions. One of the crudest examples was Thatcher's adoption of the cliché, 'There is no alternative', a blatant attempt at reordering reality to accord with the destructive anarchy of capital. But, of course, there is an alternative; quite apart from Bolshevik socialism, so effectively snuffed out by Stalin, it is important to recall that about half of the world's population lives outside, or is excluded from, capital's modes of production. Much of that half lives in acute poverty engendered by the massively exploitative and extractive nature of state economies, constructed in the wake of colonialism and of capital's exploitative wars. Mészáros has pointed out that '[i]n China one can speak of relatively small enclaves ... under the overall political control of the non-capitalist Chinese state'. He goes on to say that substantial proportions of the populations of South East Asia, Indonesia, Africa and much of Latin America must be added to the overwhelming majority of the Chinese people to make up the numbers dependent on subsistence production. In view of this, he remarks that to 'talk in front of them about the "sovereign market" would sound like a joke in bad taste'.[11] Our point here is not to propose some fanciful return to a kind of Chestertonian Distributism, it is merely to make, again, the point we have returned to so often in this book, that the market is actually incapable of resolving the problem of poverty.

The dilemma for INGOs and, for that matter, for relatively well-inclined social democracies like the present Scandinavian states and The Netherlands, is that all programmes and projects of development and humanitarian assistance have their origins from within the mores of the free market. Not only does the contradiction inherent in trying to incorporate the world's poor into the free market immediately become apparent, particularly since it is open to the charge of neo-colonialism, but, as we have tried to make clear, the concept of sustainability becomes curiously suspect. It is reasonable to see attempts at the resolution of this dilemma in the determination of ministries of development and their attendant

NGOs to concentrate on communal programmes – sustainability has also been modified to that end. Eade and Williams remark that 'people and organisations and their projects cannot be condemned if they prove unable to withstand pressures beyond their control'.[12] Many of those 'pressures' are consequences of free-market anarchy, even some which come in the form of 'natural' disasters may turn out to be triggered by the industrialised world's excessive consumption of fossil fuels and the consequent greenhouse gases which create dramatic and frequently catastrophic changes in climate.

A great deal of development work and humanitarian assistance is devoted to facilitating, creating and restoring livelihoods. INGO advertisements suggesting that if we 'give a man a fish his hunger will be stayed, but give him a net and he will feed his family/the neighbourhood etc.' are familiar enough and, up to a point, correct. Resource bases for livelihoods are frequently scarce, particularly among dispossessed and war-battered people; also, we might add, among those battered by the orthodoxies of the IMF and the World Bank. Enabling people to look after themselves, to re-establish some form of economic activity, is clearly an important objective. Such communities are not, however, castaways, they exist as part of a wider society and the issue of what becomes of them and their reclaimed livelihoods cannot totally be ignored. Nor, ultimately, is it met by pietistic exclamations that whatever follows from those reclaimed livelihoods is a matter for those who, in some discourses, are called the 'beneficiaries'.[13] Participation, consultation and so on are important issues, but they still flow from the intervention of development programmes, their resources and workers who inevitably bring their own understandings and agendas to what they do. To disclaim at least partial responsibility for the wider consequences of designing programmes or projects, of collaborating with particular communities, or of facilitating the establishment of particular resource bases, is merely to be disingenuous. Once again, the most extreme example of such disingenuousness was seen in the activities of so many, though by no means all, NGOs in Rwanda and former Zaïre (Democratic Republic of the Congo). That example was of humanitarian assistance, but, quite apart from the intimate relationship between relief and development, many of the NGOs operating in the Great Lakes region undertake both.

That humanitarian assistance is, by its very nature, *un*sustainable is an aphorism among those engaged in it: but the more careful analysis offered by Eade and Williams points to those ways in which it is not only closely linked to development, but also to what sustainability might actually mean in relief.[14] Humanitarian assistance is notoriously affected by media coverage; we need only to think of the extent to which governments were anxious to be seen to act in Kosovo while ignoring the horrors perpetrated in Sierra Leone. In this area in particular, governments, in pacifying their electorates' demands for action stimulated by news coverage (widely known as the 'CNN effect'), increasingly fund independent operations by NGOs.[15] Many of those operations are designed, not so much to meet real needs, but to satisfy needs recognised by a television-watching public.[16] There is little difficulty in seeing, in this phenomenon, the politicisation of humanitarian assistance, but politicisation goes much further. Virtually all of the world's extended crises involve continuous or sporadic violent conflict and any intervention on behalf of those affected by war has an immediate political effect. Military and political authorities in control of regions in which assistance is needed bolster their war-chests by levying taxes, in cash or in kind, on delivery. They also do their utmost to prevent assistance from reaching vulnerable people in the territories controlled by their opponents. Donors, as we have observed, inject their own politics in the choice of theatres in which to get engaged, but they may also attach strings to their aid. Emergencies frequently continue for several decades and in those circumstances UN agencies and INGOs can almost become surrogate government departments, especially in the fields of welfare, transport and infrastructure. Since assistance is given not just to bandage wounds, but to help in the restoration of normal society, political conditions (for example, demands for civil rights) may be imposed and, particularly when the IMF is involved, so may economic conditions in the form of structural adjustment policies and the reduction of tariffs and the removal of protectionist measures.[17]

It is not difficult to see how these comments are also applicable to programmes of development, even if those vast and profitable enterprises, which ministries of finance and departments of trade are apt to call 'development' projects, are dismissed from consideration. UN agencies are political by nature and their activities are ultimately subject to the vagaries of the Security Council, effectively the US. Development workers and their INGOs must normally navigate around the economic regimes imposed by the World Bank and its associates and the IMF; they must increasingly deal with the alarming rules of the WTO. Such navigation is itself a political mine-field and one of the better examples may be seen in the Philippines, a neo-colony ever since 1946 when the US granted it 'independence'. Following World War II, the Philippine economy was in ruins and US economic relief was made dependent on allowing substantial US military bases to be built, on massive concessions to US businesses and on tying the *peso* to the US dollar. All governments since the election of President Diosdado Macapagal (1962), including the fero-cious military rule of Ferdinand Marcos, have been installed with the approval of the US. Both Spanish and the subsequent US colonisa-tion had introduced a plantation economy and a large landless peasantry. At independence, land reform was an urgent necessity, but scarcely probable in the cosy neo-colonial relationship between US business and Filipino élites. That failure led directly to the peasant rising in Central Luzon which has, despite substantial inter-vention by the CIA, in tandem with an increasingly radical trade-union movement, rumbled on until today. In place of land reform, exploitative plantation owners used their profits to finance new industries which were largely tied to US companies. When, in the early 1960s, the *peso* was unhitched from the dollar, profits were repatriated to the US in a move financed by a huge loan from the IMF. Structural adjustment followed and, as at least one author has noted, one of the first neo-liberal economies was introduced.[18] By 1997, with a population of seventy-one million, its external debt amounted to over US$45 billion, roughly 53 per cent of its GNP. Burkina Faso (54.3 per cent), Sri Lanka (51.2 per cent), Uganda (56.5 per cent) and Zimbabwe (58.5 per cent) all have similar degrees of indebtedness in relation to their GNPs and, although they are by no means the worst cases,[19] they are all regarded as highly indebted countries. In 1997, official development assistance for the Philippines amounted to only US$689 million, but this is still a substantial sum.[20]

Oxfam is among the agencies working there in development; its three principal activities involve helping the indigenous people of Mindanao to find new livelihoods following the loss of their territories to loggers, assisting in the management of coastal resources (particularly in establishing commercial possibilities for in-shore fishing) and promoting education. All of these are very important for the immediate wellbeing of the vulnerable communities the organisation is setting out to help and we may be certain that, between Oxfam and the communities themselves, much will be achieved. Nonetheless, it is necessary to bear in mind the context in which this work is going on. The Filipino ruling élites are tied completely to the coat tails of the US economy, a position enshrined in the central policy statement of the US government's principal instrument for aid to overseas development, USAID:

> USAID's role is to help the country become a model Newly Industrialised Country (NIC). Our US–Philippines partnership for democracy and development is a shared commitment to mutual economic interest, democracy, and a common concern for global issues of environmental degradation, population and the AIDS epidemic.[21]

Dispossessing peasant farmers in the interests of logging,[22] or of enhanced mango farming, among other crops, for the international market has driven increasing numbers to the coasts in search of work. Pressure on the coasts has resulted in the massive destruction of mangroves which, in turn, has damaged not only in-shore fishing, but also the spawning grounds for many other deep-sea stocks. Over-fishing in the nearby seas is also reducing the capacity of coastal dwellers to maintain their livelihoods.

Recent and continuing upheavals in the Asian stock markets have further damaged an economy already enfeebled by generations of exploitation and plundering by the ruling parties. Even though the arch-plunderer Marcos has gone, his successors Aquino, Ramos and Estrada, have all maintained his ruinous fiscal policies. USAID's statement continues:

> The Philippine economy has suffered significantly from the feedback effects of the regional financial crisis, but the Government of the Philippines ... has maintained a basic commitment to liberal trade and investment policies.

That 'shared commitment to mutual economic interest' begins to have an ominous ring. The continued effort to transform the Philippines into another satellite of neo-liberal economic structures (in essence, of the TNCs) will increase the pressure on those whose lives and livelihoods cannot be incorporated into that industrialisation. Oxfam is to be commended for being among those willing to pick up the pieces when people's lives are shattered by the progress of 'liberal trade and investment policies', but experience tells us that the need for this first-aid will increase. Not only will the need increase, but so, too, will the pressure on the few resources left to the vulnerable poor. The indigenous people of Mindanao were driven from their forests in the interests of logging and commercial farming; what will happen when the diminishing resources of the coastal people are thought also to be necessary to the building of a NIC? For donors of development assistance to insist that implementing agencies should ensure that the livelihoods they facilitate should be 'sustainable' becomes, in this context, another jest in poor taste.

We have said that our arguments should not go towards the abandonment of projects of development and humanitarian assistance, but they may serve as a ground for rejecting the current sterile discussions of sustainability. In the three central chapters of this book we have described the ways in which we bring our own agendas both to the analysis and to the practice of all forms of aid. To a considerable, though more limited, degree, those agendas also determine what we mean when we use the adjective 'sustainable'. Assistance is offered to those in need, but there are two ways in which it is not always clear who these people, or societies, are. One may be seen in the dams to be built in India and Turkey to which we have already referred. Despite the claims made by the respective governments for immeasurable future benefits, all that is known for certain is who will be seriously harmed by aid for these projects; this has not prevented either state from enlisting unspecified citizens living in poverty in support of their plans. The other comes in attempts to 'target' aid towards oppressed women, the poorest or some other category of the needy without too much prior analysis of the complexity of the situation to be addressed. There may be very good reasons for *a priori* targeting, but the danger is that it seems often to become a substitute for political observation.

Many of those working in the field entertain, often only partly articulated, a not wholly disreputable model for development practice: a community in need is consulted about its problems and the ways in which it feels that these may successfully be resolved. Consultation may be augmented by providing practical assistance in basic resources and expertise which may be lacking in the community itself; the end result will be one desired by the community, will be their creation and will be enabled to survive by the efforts either of the community itself or in collaboration with its state bureaucracy. In the last two decades, much attention has been given to needs analysis; some results have been significant (we have already referred to the work of Ben Wisner), others a little fanciful. The general result of these enquiries has been to enhance the process of getting people to specify their own needs and so substantially to democratise development, at least in theory if not always in practice. Increasingly, throughout these two debates, the more enlightened donor governments have been insisting that the primary objective of all development work must be the alleviation of poverty. This has given rise to an entirely new question about how poverty is to be assessed.

It is the oddest of all questions in development theory, since it is not about poverty as those who are poor may see it, but about bourgeois capitalism's ability to recognise it. Defining absolute poverty by that well-known and widely used criterion of those living at, or below, US$1.00 a day has become suspect because of the number of communities which live without acute want, but also without using much, if any, cash. It is a crude measurement in other ways, since it cannot distinguish between more or less successful communities and those which are threatened; nor can it cover the myriad and mutually reinforcing social and personal deprivations attendant on poverty and which are only indirectly to do with consumption. Nevertheless, many professionals in development feel that it is necessary to find some fairly standard form of measurement and much research and several national and international conferences will be devoted to it. The Overseas Development Institute (ODI) has produced a useful guide to the present state of the discussion, its author adding the terse comment that 'measuring poverty is not the same as understanding why it occurs. Interventions need to tackle causes not symptoms.'[23]

We mention this debate because it springs, in part, from social-democratic anxiety about social exclusion, a phenomenon experienced by the poor in most contemporary societies. The anxiety arises on the one hand because history is littered with the bloody consequences of ignoring the socially excluded and, on the other, because capitalism, of its nature, depends on a process which socially excludes – the inane 'Third Way' is a tinselly attempt at concealing this reality. It all brings us back to the fundamental contradiction: the capitalist states see, partly out of self-interest and partly out of a sort of philanthropy, a need to ameliorate the condition of those in the most dire poverty. For this purpose it is necessary to identify the truly destitute and to help them a little way along the road to capital accumulation. In contemporary theory, 'sustainable livelihoods' are those which enable people to fend for themselves and, above all, to trade with others, yet, as it has been pointed out *ad nauseam*, capital already controls 80 per cent of world trade and is, through its current agreements, struggling to control as much as possible of the remainder. What, then, are we to make of 'sustainability'?

In our attempt to unpick the assumptions that we make about social justice, we suggested that by shifting the argument from individual to society, we could live with Glaucon's position, so long as we understood that the competing or 'bargaining' parties, postulated by philosophers from Socrates to Rawls, were not individuals, but classes. Marx wrote, in a general sort of way, about the inevitable changes in the nature of capitalism[24] and in the nature of responses to it. Lacking a crystal ball, he left those who would live to see the changes both to describe later forms of capitalism and to organise opposition to them. Classical Marxists, for so long inhibited by the corrupting effects of Stalin's reign and the United States' Cold War, failed either to recognise the changes or to understand what they meant in defining a proletariat. We cannot engage here in that particular debate, but we have already remarked that the globalisation of finance capital has enormously enlarged the working class (or, more properly, classes) in ways inconceivable in the days of the dominance of industrial capital.

What bedevils the argument is a false corollary; it is sometimes supposed, usually by our opponents, that those of us who adopt this view of class have some romantic belief in the natural wisdom of the people. When popular choice seems unfortunate, as in the fundamentalism of the Democratic Unionist Party of Northern Ireland or of Afghani militants, or in a scramble for the 'benefits' of modern capitalism, it is held up as some evidence against the validity of class definition. But it does not follow that membership of the working class automatically produces political enlightenment; that can only arise from long-term experience of a battle whose lines are still being drawn. In any case, however popular consciousness is to be described, it is infinitely variable, unlike the more slavish habits of Western intellectuals. That variability includes the multiform accounts of justice, each conditioned, but not necessarily determined, by the cultural worlds inhabited by their holders. Nevertheless, in fighting direct oppression whether physical, economic or both, any achievements, even defeats, will modify common understanding. Successes will also modify capitalism, though whether to the point of its destruction is another issue to be resolved only in the future.

Our purpose in that digression is to draw up a loose framework for considering responses in development and humanitarian assistance. We have repeatedly remarked that any conception of development which is consciously directed towards the incorporation of those involved into the contemporary web of capitalist exchange is not only doomed to futility, but is a positive encouragement to capital's exploitation of those so incorporated. Helping people by facilitating their recovery or their necessary extension of livelihoods or in their attempts at improving their environment or services is an entirely different matter. So, too, is providing assistance for those struggling to survive either a sudden emergency or a chronic and violent crisis. On the other hand, doing these things in support of the economic adventurism of, for example, the IMF is plainly unacceptable. It is here that the rub for many INGOs occurs, not the least because they are partly dependent on funds from the members of the IMF and of other, similar, international organisations.

The 'origin and the nature of justice'[25] has consistently been seen, since Glaucon's discussion with Socrates, as a matter of bargaining. Glaucon merely presented the reality of the bargaining process, one which idealist philosophers, particularly since Kant, have unsuccessfully tried to escape by constructing some abstract principle of 'fairness'. We have explained why we think that such a position in response to Glaucon's objection is inept and that social justice, whatever it may come to mean, can only be achieved by working classes which force it from a recalcitrant capitalist class. Even modest success in such an enterprise will radically alter the nature of capitalism. Major successes could result in its destruction, particularly because it is such an unstable, even anarchic, system. It would be idle to speculate about what could replace capitalism or, come to that, current accounts of social justice. Despite its instability, capital has, in the past, frequently demonstrated its capacity to adapt, but it always did so, and must always do so, by expanding the scope of its destructive competitiveness – we do not suppose it has yet reached the end of that road.

Our part is to ensure that interventions of development and humanitarian assistance are made in the interests of what we understand by social justice. The present authors maintain that the dilemma presented by programmes of development and assistance which, in one form or another, support the mores of capital, must be faced, since no matter what minimal improvements they may bring they cannot be socially just. Not only must it be faced by critics like us for whom such an exercise may not be life threatening, but by INGOs for whom it may be just that. If the sustainability of any given project or programme is dependent on its being socially just, Glaucon's question compels us to ask whose justice is at issue, just as the recognition that economic and environmental sustainability depend on whose political and cultural choices are used as a measure.

Despite our rejection of the claim advanced by some NGOs that they either constitute, or are elements of, some sort of civil society within the state, or in relation to groups of states, there is a sense in which they may become political organisations of opposition and vehicles of revolutionary change. To fulfil this role, they have, obviously enough, to be controlled by their grass-roots memberships, rather than by the managerial, oligarchic and, hence, unaccountable structure common among so many INGOs. Some of the best examples of democratic groups acting for fundamental change may be seen among the women's organisations of Latin America. Lynn Stephen describes one such in El Salvador;[26] it is called *Mujeres por la Dignidad y la Vida* (DIGNAS, Women for Dignity and Life) and emerged, during the 1990s, from the five revolutionary parties which made up the FMLN (Farabundo Martí Front for National Liberation). Establishing itself as an autonomous political organisation open to all women, it has fought for that autonomy, for diversity and for completely participatory democracy. It has devolved its structure to municipal level so that women may create their own local political platforms:

> In the municipality of Victoria, for example, local women created a political platform that includes demands for electricity, potable drinking water, education, responsible fatherhood, healthcare, housing, and an end to violence against women. In their scope, the demands ... suggest a fusion between practical and strategic gender interests.

Stephen points to the importance of that fusion since it overcame the ideological gap between the organisers who were urban, educated and, sometimes, middle-class women and the large rural membership. Collectively they have forged not only a new understanding of feminism, which allows for a variety of meanings, but a new form of socialist political action which does not depend on the emergence of a vanguard rigidly drawn only from an urban working class.

Similar movements have emerged in other parts of Latin America: the Rural Women Workers' movement of southern Brazil, the Women's Regional Council of the National Council of the Urban Popular Movement in Mexico and, in Chile, where most seasonal fruit pickers are women, the Seasonal Workers' Union, are all, in their differing ways, women's revolutionary political NGOs. The phenomenon is not, of course, confined to Latin America and although, for a variety of historical and cultural reasons, women's groups have established themselves as politically the most radical, they are not all women's organisations. They exist in many 'developing' countries and what they have in common is a democratic and participatory political formation which is intensely subversive of the political and economic programmes on offer from the contemporary imperialism of the 'developed' world. This is put a little more delicately in a brief account, by Arthur MacEwan, Professor of Economics at the University of Massachusetts, of radical progress in Kerala: 'the strong popular movements that have been the basis for the social successes do not provide the most attractive ambience for business investment'.[27] Pressures to conform to the demands of 'business investment' may frequently be irresistible, but recent history shows that no matter what the defeats, these subversive organisations continue to come into being. The present authors see them as one modern embodiment of the class struggle described by Marx and Engels. Even though they are sizeable national organisations they are, of course, smaller and less powerful than most INGOs, but they are also significantly different from them in structure and purpose. Fully democratic, their purpose is to resist exploitation by the ruling agents of capital and to bring working people together in a new politics designed to preserve diversity and to make decent living standards universal.

The growth of INGOs, despite significant internal differences in structure and international governance, has been accompanied by the growth of their rejection of the Enlightenment Project and its associated Modernity. They prize the local, but do not place it in the global. We have not, in our discussion, either of environment or of economics, dealt with this rejection which is sometimes referred to as a literature of political ecology.[28] One of the reasons for this omission is that we are uncomfortable with the concept of political ecology, preferring instead the more robust expression 'political economy of environment and development'. But a more central reason is that we think that the emphasis on agency in political ecology, and the neglect of nuanced analysis of structure, ends up as narrative rather than analysis. For that reason, and because such arguments are increasingly advanced by INGOs, it is worth dealing with political ecology as a separate issue.

All the signposts – 'post-modern', 'post-development', 'post-structuralist' – are to be found in the literature promoting the concept of political ecology and, in it, language and discourse replace, to a considerable degree, the political, leaving only the cultural environment. Escobar, who is a leading proponent of it, illustrates this in the subtitles of Chapters 2 to 5 of his book *Encountering Development*, each of which begins with 'The Tale … ' or 'Tales of … '.[29] The arguments and critiques produced by political ecologists are, of course, founded on more than discourse analysis and frequently revolve around an anti-modern, anti-structural axis.[30] The theory's practical application is, perhaps, best demonstrated by the INGO *Médecins sans Frontières* (MSF) which insists, with some justification, on partiality and on humanitarian rights – thus challenging the traditional view that neutrality must be maintained and the sovereignty of the state respected, including its monopoly of violence. But the political argument for MSF's position is vitiated precisely by its unaccountability or, in other words, its complete lack of democratic structures or responses. At a fundamental level, it is actually contemptuous of democratic structure which it identifies as an impediment to the efficient fulfilment of its mission. It is the best example of the INGO chevalier culture which allows it to charge over any hill, anywhere and at any time. It is not altogether surprising that the equally messianic culture of the Nobel committee ensured that MSF was the INGO awarded the Peace Prize.

Watts and McCarthy argue that two interpretations of the crises in development are used to attack both neo-liberalism and Marxism and to build political ecology. They are, respectively, theories of anti-development and impasse theory.[31] Anti-development theory rejects a Western modernity and its associated forms of rationality. It rejects the alliance between state and science but fails to account for the biggest influence, private capital, which after all drives the system. Much as dons dislike the thought, not least because it attacks their sinecures and their monopolies of research funds gained through peer reviews, most science research is conducted and financed by private capital. A glance at job advertisements in *New Scientist* would confirm our argument. The present authors are inclined to see the emergence of political ecology as a defence mechanism for wounded donnish and, indeed, in the case of the INGOs, wounded philanthropic sensibilities. Apropos of the latter, we should remember the charge levelled against philanthropy by Marx and Engels, that it serves only 'to secure the continued existence of bourgeois society'.[32]

Most importantly, anti-development-cum-anti-structural theory throws aside the great gains that have been achieved by many poorer countries, like the rapid decreases in morbidity and mortality. It replaces the Marxist view of capital accumulation and its accompanying production of class with a populist account of the social spectacle. Its theoreticians reject Marxist analysis on the ground that it has reached an impasse in failing to resolve the issues of poverty. In its place they reassert complexity and diversity as primary analytical categories (and are thus profoundly anti-state), they also stress the importance of classless movements from below in which micropolitics address local and specific problems and dispense with any macro-political analysis and, crucially, action. Politics becomes what Nairn describes as 'corporate populism' of the kind espoused by

Blair.[33] It is on to this fertile ground that the INGOs walk, bringing with them their appropriate technology and participatory approaches, rejecting politics but distributing nuanced placebos. This is discourse analysis in practice; it rejects metanarrative to tell no story, except to offer local culture as a countervailing bunker. Such subjectivity, which offers local autonomy as the bulwark against globalisation, is essentially a debate about, not a contribution to, development. It is a story that can illustrate agency but says nothing about the structural violence meted out by capital's uneven development.

In our use of illustrative material in this book, we have been selective in our choice of indigenous NGOs. INGOs normally work with partner organisations in the 'field' and are equally selective in their choice preferring, wherever possible, to deal with like-minded groups. We have chosen, as our examples, organisations which have understood that sustainable micro-political solutions are possible only in those situations where equal attention is paid to modifying the macro-political institutions. Achieving successful development is a battle to be fought on both fronts or, as Guattari has expressed it: 'A political analysis ... should be inseparable from a politics of analysis.'[34] In suggesting this, Guattari seems partly to have abandoned the position that he took with Gilles Deleuze in their book *Capitalisme et schizophrénie*. In it they advocated an understanding, similar to the one we have described as belonging to INGOs, in which a collection of micro-political acts combine in their overall force to compel change in macro-political structures, without the need for macro-political theory. Our principal charge against that view is the same as our charge against INGO theory – any rejection of macro-political analysis will, at the best, allow the survival and adaptation of the exploitative *status quo* or, at worst, encourage the resurgence of fascism.

INGOs will only enjoy a sustainable future if they recognise that it can only be as allies of the disadvantaged in that struggle. So long as they are simply the palliative arms of those states actually creating poverty, even if only through the medium of their markets and TNCs, or if they are fundamentally the agencies of genocidal and terrorist states (British and US actions in Iraq spring to mind[35]), then INGOs lack political and social credibility. It becomes necessary to ask whether or not they are sustainable. As they are constituted at present, they can offer substantial support for communities whose livelihoods are threatened or destroyed and for those whose existence is jeopardised by disaster of whatever kind. They are capable of doing this in a wide variety of ways and the value of what they do should not be underestimated, even though their reach is inevitably limited. Wherever possible they work in partnership with the states in which they operate and, increasingly, in partnership with UN bodies, particularly in the case of humanitarian assistance. Relationships of this kind inevitably lend the presence of INGOs in any given community a certain political profile. The partnership model may also extend to indigenous NGOs, some of which may even be created to fit needs which flow from the activities and international relationships of the development or humanitarian agencies. Local NGOs are incorporated into the organisation and the culture which comes into being as a consequence of a complex presence of one, or more, INGOs and international agencies, but the relationship is unequal – a point that has frequently been remarked. Indigenous groups do not control the purse strings, they are usually unable to take part in the planning and deliberations in the headquarters of INGOs and agencies and, where trained personnel are at issue, they are often thin on the ground in a heavily indebted country.[36] An INGO's choice of local NGO partners is often made managerially and the relationship is frequently one of patronage. Examples of INGO contempt for indigenous NGOs, both among the elected and the rejected, are legion.

Some of the more enlightened INGOs are well aware of the problems and are making valiant efforts to solve them, but solutions produced by undemocratic management to what are essentially political difficulties will always be defective. Since all interventions by INGOs are political events, it not only becomes necessary for political self-analysis to take place within each organisation, but it is also necessary to understand, finally to emulate, the political agendas and structures of movements like DIGNAS. Theorists and workers in development and in humanitarian assistance have long campaigned for all projects to be assessed by the criteria of sustainability. We no longer expect social-democratic states to abandon their attachment to capital or to the development agendas and definitions of sustainability involved in that attachment. If, on the other hand, INGOs are to become sustainable they must wean themselves from their dependence on those states and from their oligarchic structures of management and engage, instead, in the complexity of the socio-political programmes advanced by the organisations of the poor. For the issue of poverty and all its ramifications to be addressed, INGOs, like the rest of us, must engage with, and in, macro-politics. Such an engagement will involve them in abandoning their privileged position as state dependants and in a complete reversal of their present mores. Like the highly politicised women's movements in Latin America and elsewhere, they will have to learn to combat capital, its structures and its governments.

Notes

Chapter 1

1. 'When the rich wage war it's the poor who die', *The Devil and the Good God*, act 1.
2. Goldman, 1998.
3. His quotation is from Hadaway's *Modest-Witness 'Second Millennium, Female Man Once a House'*.
4. Holdgate, M.W., Kassas, M. and White, G.F., 1982.
5. Glacken, 1967.
6. Hoskins, 1955.
7. Thompson, 1980.
8. Turner, *et al.*, 1994.
9. The most spirited recent defence of the phrase known to the present authors is offered by Ash Narain Roy, 1999. In it he urges an economic coalition between Third World countries which collectively could resist the depredations of the dominant economic alliances.
10. The present authors have themselves, when faced with the need for an acceptable collective noun, used the expression in their last book, Middleton and O'Keefe, 1998.
11. Middleton, O'Keefe and Moyo, 1993.
12. Fowler, 1997, 6–8.
13. Hill, 1992, 266–7.
14. Pelling, 1976, 173–8, see also Hobsbawm, 1969.
15. *Ibid.*, 31 ff., 54 ff.
16. Mill, 1998.
17. 'Economic and Philosphical Manuscripts', Marx, 1975.
18. 'The Role of Voluntary Organizations in Development: A Concept Paper', L.D. Brown and D.C. Korten, Boston: Boston Institute for Development Research, 1989.
19. Wahab, in Blunt and Warren, 1996, 56.

20. We shall return to this agreement in Chapter 3. The MAI has now been transferred to the WTO and, despite its temporary defeat in Seattle, will undoubtedly re-emerge in some suitably sanitised form.
21. Recently, and improbably, rebranded as State Peace and Development Council (SPDC).
22. Galeano, 1997, see, in particular, 135–9 and 215–19.
23. The worldwide crumbling of weaker economies, Mexico and most of the rest of Latin America, the South East Asian 'tigers' and Russia are all cases in point. Japan's ills are largely self-inflicted but they, too, point up the short-termism and simple avarice of ordinary capitalist enterprise.
24. Luttwak, Edward, 'Why Blame the Russians?', *London Review of Books*, 20 (18), 17 September 1998.
25. Mészáros, 1995, see Chapter 4.4.2.
26. See, in particular, 'The Chapter on Capital' section one, 250–374 in Marx, 1973 and Chapters 7 and 9 in Marx, 1976.
27. Wahab, 1996, 56.
28. For an impassioned and well-argued support for this view see George and Sabelli, 1994.
29. One of the most honourable examples may be seen in Escobar, 1995. It is a book in which the author's progressive political choices lie at odds with his espousal of a reactionary philosophy.
30. Peet and Watts, 1996, 3.
31. WCED, 1987.
32. Quoted in Tabb, William K., in 'Progressive Globalism: Challenging the Audacity of Capital', *Monthly Review*, 50 (9), February, 1999.
33. See UNDP, in most years. See also the remarks on the increase in child malnutrition in UNICEF, 1998.

Chapter 2

1. 1685–1732 – these lines are taken from a collection of his Fables, published posthumously in 1738.
2. Glaciers, of course, occasionally crack very suddenly. We may recall the convulsions of the British broadsheets whenever the Delegates of the Clarendon Press authorise a new dictionary – the fuss around the publication of *The New Oxford English Dictionary* in 1998 was a case in point.
3. For those unacquainted with this phenomenon, we attach this well-known example: a simple syllogism like all As are B, C is an A, therefore C is B (all people are mortal, C is a person, therefore C is mortal) can be mistakenly constructed thus: all As are B, C is B, therefore C is an A (all people are mortal, C is mortal, therefore C is a person where, in fact, C is Fido, the pet dog).
4. English professional philosophers, in Carroll's day, were largely unaffected by the philosophical upheavals brought about by the French Revolution, particularly among the German idealists. Yet these ideas

found their way among British intellectuals chiefly as a consequence of Darwin's work. In Oxford of the time, it is interesting to notice J.H. Newman's early attachment to Darwinism (see Cameron, 1967) which obviously influenced his *Essay on the Development of Christian Doctrine* (1845) and played a role in the University's seismic convulsions around the Tractarian movement.

5.   Nietzsche, 1996, 13. The authors are indebted to Deleuze, 1983, for this reading of Nietzsche.

6.   McCabe, 1985, 124.

7.   Jacques Derrida introduced the notion of 'deconstruction' to philosophy. His most important early book discussing the question was published in English as *Writing and Difference*, 1978. Jean-François Lyotard is a well-known contemporary exponent of post-modernism; his principal book is *La Condition postmoderne*, 1979, published in English as *The Postmodern Condition: A Report on Knowledge*, 1984.

8.   There is a substantial philosophical and theological literature, forming a large part of the development of European thought, which deals with the question of the primacy of faith over reason. Among the most significant writers are John Scotus Eriugena (*c.* 810–877 AD), Anselm of Canterbury (*c.* 1033–1109 AD), Albert the Great (*c.* 1193–1280 AD) who was also the teacher of the most important of them all, Thomas Aquinas (*c.* 1225–74 AD). There are many more.

9.   Wittgenstein, 1922, in particular paragraphs 6.423–7. The last of these is the much quoted aphorism: 'Whereof one cannot speak, thereof one must be silent.'

10. Marx, 1975. Since Marx's critique was confined to Third Part (iii) 'The State', it is entitled 'Critique of Hegel's Doctrine of the State' in the edition we have used.

11. Vološinov, 1986 (edition consulted), Part 1, Chapter 3. It has been suggested that Vološinov was one of the pseudonyms used by Mikhail Bakhtin (1895–1975) writing in difficult times; this is the subject of some dispute.

12. Vološinov, 1986, 28. There are many extant works in the philosophy of language to which the interested reader may refer for an elaboration of semiotics, but another passage in Vološinov will point the way (note that 'ideology', in this passage, means simply pertaining to ideas: 'Everything ideological possesses *meaning*: it represents, depicts, or stands for something lying outside itself. In other words, it is a sign. *Without signs there is no ideology*', Vološinov, Part 1, Chapter 1, 9.

13. *Ibid.*, 27.

14. *Ibid.*, 26.

15. Marx and Engels, 1965, 41–3.

16. Ludwig Wittgenstein opens his major work, *Philosophical Investigations*, 1953, with an extensive discussion of language, but for our purposes the reader might like to refer to his preparatory work for that book, *The Blue and the Brown Books*, 1969, in which the discussion to which we

refer is set out more simply. It is necessary only to note that, in the later work, the arguments are refined, elaborated and improved.

17. 'Answering the Question: What is Postmodernism?', reproduced in Docherty, 1993.

18. For the purposes of this book we include in the phrase the World Bank, the International Monetary Fund and the World Trade Organisation.

19. *The Oxford English Dictionary*, 1971.

20. Newman, 1912, 233.

21. Mészáros, 1995, 11.

22. Gray, 1998.

23. Freire, 1972, 22.

24. Hurst and Thompson, 1996.

25. Mészáros, 1995, 37.

26. See UNDP, 1997.

27. A point made at length in UNDP, 1998.

28. See, for example, Keynes, 1973, 269–71, Harvey, 1996, Chapter 7, Hutton, 1996, 235–7, Gray, 1998, Chapter 1.

29. See, for example, *Blueprint for a Green Economy*, in which the authors, all from the London Environmental Economics Centre, made a brave, if politically misguided, attempt to adapt the cost-benefit analyses of classical economics to include environmental costs. Significantly, the *Daily Mail* hailed it as '[a] *cash-register* full of stimulating suggestions' (emphasis added).

30. There are those who argue that a political agenda formed by the end of World War II and the beginning of the Cold War was of equal, if not greater, importance than the economic imperative. See, for example, Laffan, 1996, Chapter 1 – Introduction.

31. This agreement was designed by the OECD to do for investment what GATT and the General Agreement on Trade in Services (GATS) have done for trade and services. It is international and it will prevent its signatory nations from protecting their industries, resources and financial institutions from foreign investment. Nations not at present members of the OECD will be allowed (some might say 'pressured') to enter this agreement once it has been reached. It was, perhaps, not so much abandoned by the OECD as passed on to the remit of the WTO. That organisation's Third Ministerial Conference (30 November–3 December 1999) collapsed in the face of opposition from the poorer states and from NGOs and a disenchanted public, but the MAI has not been abandoned. There are other equally destructive agreements waiting in the wings, including a wide-ranging free-trade pact between the US and the EU, but these are beyond the scope of this book. We shall examine the issues in Chapter 3.

32. In September of 1998, France withdrew from the negotiations and in October, Britain expressed its disagreement with the direction negotiators were taking. However, Britain urged a new start to the discussions while other members suggested the transfer of the whole issue to the WTO (the *Guardian*, 30 October 1998).

33. At the time of writing, March 2000, the South East Asian markets had recovered, but the effects of the collapse on the economies of many of the affected states has been, and continues to be, disastrous.

34. Ireland's banks were active in support of tax evasion through the use, by their wealthier Irish clients, of secret off-shore accounts; its beef industry extensively swindled the EU; former government ministers (including a Taoiseach (Prime Minister)) have been kept by industrialists and property developers and its parliamentary representatives award themselves pay-rises well in excess of national agreements.

35. Watkins, 1995, 112.

36. Kevin Watkins, 'Plato's Pearls Cast Before Globalist Swine', *Guardian*, 1 December 1997.

37. Jeremy Sachs, Director of the Centre for International Development, Harvard University, remarked that every major rescue attempt made by the IMF since the middle of 1977 has failed. These were Brazil (January, 1999), Russia (August, 1998), Korea (December, 1997), Indonesia (November, 1997) and Thailand (August, 1997) – *Guardian*, 16 January 1999.

38. An interesting account of Thatcher's crusade may be found in Beckett, 1998.

39. Mészáros, 1995, this phrase is the title of Chapter 2.

40. *Ibid.*

Chapter 3

1. This is expressed succinctly by Zakes Mda, 1997: 'When in our Orature the storyteller begins the story "They say it once happened ...", we are the "they". No Individual owns any story. The community is the owner of the story, and it can tell it the way it deems fit.' (12).

2. The first two chapters of Carr, 1987, give, in an entirely other context, an elegant account of the argument.

3. A critical summary of the varying forms of deep ecology may be found in Lewis, 1992, though we would take issue with his rather dated account of Marxism and, consequently, the slightly *passé* nature of the explanations he demands of it.

4. His remarks may be found in a succinct article under the heading 'romanticism, philosophical' in Honderich, 1995.

5. 'A Discourse on the Origin of Inequality' in Rousseau, 1993.

6. Hegel, 1975.

7. *The Wanderer Over the Sea of Clouds*, painted in 1818.

8. Vološinov, 1986, 83.

9. Lovelock, 1995.

10. *Ibid.*, 10.

11. *Ibid.*, emphasis added.

12. Lewis, 1992, 28.

13.   He describes them as 'anti-humanist anarchism', 'primitivism', 'humanist eco-anarchism', 'eco-marxism' and 'eco-feminism' (27).

14.   Thoreau, 1977.

15.   For example, Kate Soper has produced a concise and robust discussion of deep ecology in 'Human Needs and Natural Relations: The Dilemmas of Ecology II', published in *CNS*, 9 (1–33), March 1998. Martin W. Lewis (1992) sites this journal within the camp of eco-Marxism and, despite his suspicion of Marxism (contemporary Marxism is, *ipso facto*, 'heterodox'), seems to regard it with some respect. His own book, *Green Delusions*, contains not only some of the best summary accounts of deep ecology but also some trenchant comments. He produces them, however, against the unargued position that there is no real alternative to contemporary advanced capitalism, even though it is in need of some regulation.

16.   One of the most significant texts in the formation of deep ecology is Naes, 1989. A sympathetic, if critical, account of his work may be found in Harvey, 1996, 167–9.

17.   Carson, 1962.

18.   Ward and Dubos, 1972. The others were *The Home of Man* and *Progress for a Small Planet*.

19.   Middleton, O'Keefe and Moyo, 1993.

20.   WCED, 1987, ix.

21.   WCED, 1987.

22.   *Ibid.*, 208–17.

23.   *Ibid.*, 348.

24.   The quotation is from Maurice Strong and Mustafa Tolba, architects of the Conference. For a fuller account of the UNCED and its consequences see Middleton, O'Keefe and Moyo, 1993.

25.   Lafferty and Eckerberg, 1998.

26.   Lucy Jarosz, 'Defining Deforestation in Madagascar' in Peet and Watts, 1996, 148.

27.   World Bank, 1992, 1–24.

28.   *Ibid.*, 7–8.

29.   'It's Apocalypse Now as the World Boils Over', *Observer*, 27 February 2000.

30.   Quoted in a letter from Dr Liam J. Bannon to *The Irish Times*, 27 May 1998. The present authors have failed to verify the quotation.

31.   Harvey, 1996.

32.   *Ibid.*, 186. Harvey takes the quoted words from R. Gottlieb, *Forcing the Spring: The Transformation of the American Environmental Movement*, 1993.

33.   Harvey, 1996.

34.   *Ibid.*, 118.

35.   *Ibid.*

36.   This section of Harvey's book, despite some relatively minor reservations on our part, is of great importance. But it leads to a far more important set of ideas represented in his title as 'the Geography of Difference'.

37. Narotzky, 1997, 8.
38. This is not to suggest that Marx was not dealing, at any stage, with Leibnizian concepts since we may find a direct reference in, for example, his remarks on equality in 'On the Jewish Question', Marx, 1975.
39. Harvey, 1996, 359.
40. Escobar, 1995, 203–6.
41. WCED, 1987, 5–6.
42. Escobar, 1995, 203.
43. 'Unaccommodated Nature', CNS, 9 (3–35), September 1998.
44. Chambers, 1997.
45. Ibid., 11.
46. See the Guardian, 12 February, 1999, which told the story not only on the front page but also inside in a remarkable double-page spread.
47. Middleton, O'Keefe and Moyo, 1993, 115–19.
48. See, among very many other titles, Hill, 1988 and Whelan, 1996, for accounts of such attitudes.
49. George Monbiot, Mark Milner and John Vidal, 'Biotech Firm Has Eyes On All You Can Eat', Guardian, 15 December 1997.
50. 'Genes to Make America', Guardian, 17 December 1997.
51. Middleton and O'Keefe, 1998, 20–1.
52. GATT, 1994, Annex 1C, Articles 27–38.
53. See, for example, Vandana Shiva writing in the Guardian, 18 December 1998.
54. Middleton and O'Keefe, 1998.
55. Miguel A. Altieri, 'Ecological Impacts of Industrial Agriculture and the Possibilities for Truly Sustainable Farming', Monthly Review, 50 (3), July/August 1998.
56. One of the best, brief descriptions and analyses of this system is to be found in Michael Watts, 'Peasants Under Contract: Agri-food Complexes in the Third World' in Bernstein, Crow, Mackintosh and Martin, 1990.
57. R.C. Lewontin, 'The Maturing of Capitalist Agriculture: Farmer as Proletarian', Monthly Review, 50 (3), July/August 1998.
58. 'Escaping the deforestation mythology' in LEISA, ILEIA Newsletter, December 1996.
59. A much fuller and very useful analysis is to be found in Sogge, Biekart and Saxby, 1996. See particularly Chapter 4, 'Do Private Agencies Really Make a Difference?' by Alan Fowler and Kees Biekart. Looking at the same issue in terms not of development, but of humanitarian assistance, the present authors have argued that the greater part of humanitarian aid has to do with providing the survivors of catastrophe with a temporary welfare state rather than tackling the issues which caused the problem in the first place (see Middleton and O'Keefe, 1998).
60. This passage is taken from a brief country profile of Peru posted, probably by the CIA, on the World Wide Web.

61.   The sources for these abbreviated statistics are the World Bank's *World Development Report, 1997*, ITeM, 1995/96 and ITeM, 1997/98.
62.   Reported by Mohamed Mechergui and Gerrit van Vuren in *LEISA, ILEIA Newsletter*, July, 1988.
63.   World Bank news releases for Middle East and North Africa in 1998, 96/32 on June 13, 98/1842 on June 23, 98/1890 on July 15. Posted on the World Wide Web: www.worldbank.org
64.   An example may be found in the otherwise excellent policy document, issued in 1991 by The Netherlands' Development Cooperation Information Department of the Ministry of Foreign Affairs, entitled *A World of Difference*. See, in particular, Chapter 3 'Greater Risks', 70–6.
65.   *Guardian*, 21 October 1997.
66.   *Guardian*, 23 October 1997.
67.   *Guardian*, 6 May 1998.
68.   Osborn and Brigg, 1998, Annex 3, 78–126.

Chapter 4

1.   Max Weber once defined a 'status group' as 'a group societalised through its special styles of life, its conventional and specific notions of honour, and the economic opportunities it legally monopolises' (Weber, 1963). The appositeness of this remark will, we hope, become clear in the course of this chapter.
2.   The radical economist, Samir Amin, has written a spirited attack on economics thus conceived (Amin, 1998).
3.   From the introduction to Cole, 1995.
4.   'Historians and Economists: I' in Hobsbawm 1997, 135.
5.   Keynes, 1973, 382–3.
6.   The first of these headlines is taken from the *Guardian*, 17 April 2000, the next two come from the *Observer*, 4 October 1998.
7.   'Hedge funds' is financier's cant for a simple but dangerous phenomenon. Producers or market intermediaries would sell, or undertake to sell, some future product (say, a wheat harvest) for a fixed price but to be delivered at the date at which it became available. The purchaser would effectively be gambling on the general market price of that product at the time of delivery and sale. On the other hand the producer has hedged her or his risks of any catastrophic fall in prices. Speculators dealt widely in this kind of futures market not only by purchasing the goods in advance, but by trading in the variable value, not of the product itself, but of their investment in it, thus hedging their bets. This practice then extended to other things traded on stock markets. Market gamblers began to lay the same kinds of bet on the future value of currencies, stocks and shares, rates of interest and so on. Large investors in this kind of gambling also hedged their bets by trading in the value of what they had purchased. Three forms of purchase can operate in this baroque business. The purchaser may buy the product, share or

currency outright for the prevailing price and this is known as the 'spot' price paid in the 'spot' market. Contracting to buy but paying the price on the agreed date of purchase is dealing in 'futures'. It is also possible to take out an 'option' by paying a deposit on the purchase which is forfeited if it is not finally made. Trading in all these is common and in each version it is possible to hedge, or lay off, bets by subsequent layers of trading. Many larger financial organisations have put up enormous sums for this purpose, these are known as 'hedge funds'. Some of them are used cautiously, but many huge corporations and banks may trade 'aggressively' which simply means taking enormous risks in search of astronomic profits. It is an easily toppled house of cards and the Barings Bank crash is an example. Orthodox finance now regards them with such dread that early in 1999 measures to restrict them were announced – it is not clear that they will be effective.

8. The US determination to protect its giant fruit corporations' stake in the European banana market is a case in point. Of course, the US Administration was encouraged in this by a donation of $500,000 from one of the biggest fruit corporations to the Democrat Party's funds.

9. John Gray, 1998, has provided a succinct account of the contemporary version of this in a chapter entitled 'How Global Markets Favour the Worst Kinds of Capitalism: A New Gresham's Law?'

10. See a pre-performance account of the speech in the *Guardian*, 16 November 1998.

11. Cole, Cameron and Edwards, 1983. The present authors owe much of the formulation of this argument to the admirable account of the issues given by these three authors.

12. Cole, Cameron and Edwards, 1983, spell out the ancestry of the three theories more fully than is necessary for our purposes. They present it in tabular form on p. 16 of their book.

13. Ricardo, 1996.

14. Giddens, 1998.

15. Private communication from the author.

16. Marx, 1976, 126. Marx's quotation from Locke is taken from 'Some Considerations on the Consequences of the Lowering of Interest'.

17. *Ibid.*, 127–8.

18. *Ibid.*, 130.

19. 'Introduction' to Marx, 1976, 42.

20. Marx, 1976, 132.

21. Marx contrasts the valuable role of 'a general or a banker' with that of 'man as such [who] plays a very mean ['shabby' in the Moore & Aveling translation] part'. He refers to paragraph 190 of *Philosophy of Right* in which Hegel distinguishes roles in society from the 'composite idea which we call *man*'; it is to the latter that Hegel attributes not a 'mean' but a minor role. In giving the passage this twist Marx probably had paragraphs 199–208 in mind, in which Hegel sets out his account of class in which differences are immutable because established by nature.

22. Marx, 1976, 135.

23.   *Ibid.*, 136.
24.   Smith, 1974, see Book One, Chapter X.
25.   *Ibid.*, 238–45.
26.   Many people find Marx's work daunting, less because of its difficulty and more because of its scale, yet he wrote very well. His style is simple and attractive though, in some ways, he was poorly served by two of his translators, Samuel Moore and Edward Aveling. For those who find the extent of his major works too alarming, one of the best simplified accounts of Marx's theories of value, money and surplus-value may be found in Cole, 1995, 125–39.
27.   'What Can History Tell Us About Contemporary Society?' in Hobsbawm, 1997. Nicolai D. Kondratiev was a Russian economist who gave his name to a theory of business cycles.
28.   Reports suggest that Western tobacco companies now control 10 per cent of the huge and lucrative market in China and are fighting to take more, *Guardian*, 20 November 1998.
29.   Edward Luttwak, 'Why Blame the Russians?' *London Review of Books*, 20, (18), 17 September 1998.
30.   Hobsbawm, 1969.
31.   Marx describes the process succinctly in Marx, 1976, 580–2, though in his day, he, unlike Kondratiev, thought that cycles lasted for only ten years (790). In Vol. II of *Capital*, he also uses the term 'industrial cycle' to mean the period from investment to return in which capital valorises itself and on p. 486 makes a link between the two.
32.   Marx, 1981, 215.
33.   Two examples will serve for the many works covering the issue: Harris, 1983, and Hobsbawm, 1995.
34.   In *Woman's Own*, 31 October 1987.
35.   Marx and Engels, 1967, 83–4.
36.   World Bank, 1998/99.
37.   'The State in a Changing World: Social-Democratizing Global Capitalism?' *Monthly Review*, 50 (5), October 1998.
38.   For a simple but far fuller account of the production of surplus-value see Marx, 1976, 975–8.
39.   Hobsbawm, 1969.
40.   This process was brilliantly analysed in Braverman, 1974, and set in contemporary debate by John Bellamy Foster in his introduction to a new edition published in 1999.
41.   Will Hutton, 'Why the World's Economies Are Suffering a Glut Reaction', *Observer*, 13 December 1998.
42.   'Jitters as Oil Prices Hit $25', quoting Mark Redway, *Guardian*, 23 November 1999.
43.   'Oil Cartel Lights a Match that Could Explode the 90s Boom', *Guardian*, 2 March 2000.
44.   The Commission on Global Governance, 1995.
45.   *Ibid.*, 5.
46.   *Ibid.*, 255–6.

47. See John Vidal, 'Yes, We Have No Bananas', *Guardian*, *G2*, 18 November 1998. It was, of course, the same company which was so generous to the Democrat Party and mentioned earlier in this chapter.
48. Leo Panitch, *Monthly Review*, 50 (5), October 1998.
49. Harvey, 1996, 323.
50. *Guardian*, 3 July, 1998.
51. Charlotte Denny, 'It's All a Matter of Balance', *Guardian*, 17 November 1998.
52. Joseph K. Roberts, 'Multilateral Agreement on Investment', *Monthly Review*, 50 (5), October 1998.
53. See OECD press release, 14 December 1998 (www.oecd.org).
54. See OECD Policy Brief, No. 2, 1997 (www.oecd.org).
55. Joseph K. Roberts, *Monthly Review*, 50 (5), October 1998. Obviously Roberts is not writing about annual rates of investment, see table 4.1 for these figures.
56. Argentina, Brazil, Chile, China, Colombia, Czech Republic, Hungary, India, Indonesia, Korea Republic, Malaysia, Mexico and Thailand: China alone received 13 per cent of the total FDI for 1996.
57. Azerbaijan, Bolivia, Egypt and Turkey. For a fuller analysis of FDI, TNCs and Third World economies see Elson, 1995.
58. George Monbiot, 'Still Bent on World Conquest', *Guardian*, 16 December 1999.
59. These would include a number of economists around journals like *Antipode*, *Capital and Class*, *CNS*, *Monthly Review*, *Race and Class* and *The Review of Radical Political Economists*.
60. World Bank, 1992, 10.
61. See, for example, Hutton, 1996.
62. World Bank, 1995, 18.
63. An excellent criticism of the *World Development Report, 1997* may be found in Panitch, *Monthly Review*, 50 (5), October 1998.
64. World Bank, 1998/99, 144.
65. *Ibid.*, 4.
66. IUCN, 1980.
67. Pearce, Markandya and Barbier, 1989, xiii.
68. *Ibid.*, 2–3.
69. Pearce, 1991, 127.
70. *Ibid.*, 154–6.
71. Pearce, Markandya and Barbier, 1989, 2.
72. *Ibid.*, 34.
73. WCED, 1987, 46–52.
74. Pearce, 1991, 209–24.
75. Pearce, Barbier and Markandya, 1990, 2–11.
76. Mészáros, 1995.
77. Larry Elliott, 'Feed the World Instead', *Guardian*, 18 January 1999.
78. UNDP, 1998.
79. The authors are indebted to Arthur, 1996, and to IteM, 1997/98, for much of the information about Haiti.

80.   A complicated treaty between, on the one hand the 'Grand Alliance' of England, Spain, the Dutch Republic and the Holy Roman Emperor and, on the other France; it was aimed at restoring the colonial *status quo* prior to the War of the Grand Alliance (1689–97).
81.   James, 1980.
82.   It is estimated that his regime was responsible for 40,000 murders, his principal instruments in this carnage were the infamous *Tonton-Macoutes* (IteM, 1997/98).
83.   Arthur, 1996, 152–3.
84.   Frederick J. Conway in Conroy and Litvinoff, 1988.
85.   Arthur, 1996, 152.
86.   Andy Merrifield, 'Class Formation, Capital Accumulation, and the Downsizing of America', *Monthly Review*, 51 (5), October 1999. See Marx, 1976, Chapter 25, pt. 2 and Marx and Engels, 1967.

Chapter 5

1.   'Man's capacity for justice makes democracy possible, but man's inclination to injustice makes democracy necessary.' Reinhold Niebuhr, *Children of Light and Children of Darkness*, 1944.
2.   Plato, 1974, see 66–73.
3.   In *System of Economic Contradictions: or the Philosophy of Poverty*, 1864 (not consulted).
4.   Karl Marx, 28 December 1846. Letter to P.V. Annenkov, quoted in Tucker, 1978. Marx wrote a much fuller criticism of Proudhon in *The Poverty of Philosophy*, 1847, first published in English in 1900.
5.   Marx, 1973.
6.   Marx, 1976, see, in particular, 163–77.
7.   Mészáros, 1995, 108, see 108–9.
8.   A recent article by Michael Byers suggests that existing nation states are increasingly rendered redundant by the globalisation of capital. He suggests that NGOs, both local and international, but particularly the latter, are replacing them as the oppositional 'civil society' facing the combined power of TNCs. This is a popular argument, particularly among crusading, but unaccountable, NGOs, which we refute on two grounds. Not only is TNC capital increasingly, and by its nature, unstable, but it is dependent on existing state structures both to facilitate its activities and as precarious anchors in the financial storms it creates. 'Woken Up in Seattle', *London Review of Books*, 6 January 2000, 22 (1).
9.   More formally known as *North-South: A Programme for Survival* (1980) and *Common Crisis* (1983), they were produced by the Independent Commission on International Development Issues (ICIDI) which was chaired by Willy Brandt who, from 1969 to 1974, had been Chancellor of the former Federal German Republic (West Germany).
10.   A sophisticated, neo-Kantian version of this position may be found in Hare, 1952.

11.   Among the best examples we may consider *Rerum Novarum*, Leo XIII in 1981, *Qadragesimo Anno*, Pius XI in 1931, *Pacem in Terris*, John XXIII in 1963, *Laborem exercens* 1981, and *Sollicitudo rei socialis* 1987, both from John-Paul II.
12.   Nietzsche, 1996, 61.
13.   Foucault, 1991, 84.
14.   From W.S. Gilbert, *The Mikado*.
15.   Hugo Adam Bedau, in Honderich, 1995, 732.
16.   In this context it is, nonetheless, interesting to note the refusal, by many major European donors and the US, to fund the re-establishment of Rwanda's apparatus of retributive justice and its infrastructure following the genocide. This refusal did not prevent Western governments, newspapers and some NGOs from belabouring the Rwandan government for its failure to administer justice quickly enough to those arrested for participating in the slaughter.
17.   It should be obvious that in this book, and in the two earlier works on which we have collaborated, we make political judgements which could easily and alternatively be subsumed either under religious precept or retributive justice.
18.   *OED*.
19.   Thomas Nagel, in Honderich, 1995, 248–9. Nagel, in his valuable survey of the problems, expresses the abstraction a little differently: 'people who are similarly situated in morally relevant respects should be treated similarly'.
20.   John Rawls is a major figure in contemporary social and political philosophy. He taught at Cornell and Harvard and his publication, in 1971, of *A Theory of Justice* has hugely influenced all subsequent debate on the matter.
21.   Rawls, 1971, 11–17.
22.   Rawls, 1996, see, particularly, 15–22.
23.   Rawls, 1971, 148–9.
24.   Brian Barry is Professor of Political Science at the London School of Economics and has worked extensively to bring public policy, political theory and philosophy together. *Theories of Justice* is a major examination of the theories advanced by David Hume and Rawls and is a major contribution to the work of the latter.
25.   Barry, 1989.
26.   Plato, § 358–9, 104, also quoted in Barry, 1989, 6.
27.   Barry, 1989, 17.
28.   Barry points out that analysis of this position is helped by the use of a mathematical solution, proposed by J.F. Nash in 1950, to a problem in the theory of bargaining. Calling it 'the Nash solution', he demonstrates its capacity to illuminate the ways in which bargaining (no matter how indirect) may produce the 'most that parties could hope for' in a given process. See, in particular, 12–49.
29.   Barry, 1989, 6.
30.   See Nietzsche, 1997, Book 2, ¶ 97, 59.

31. Barry, 1989, 282–8.
32. *Ibid.*, 288–9. The quotation is taken from Adam Smith's *The Theory of Moral Sentiments.*
33. Barry distinguishes between impartiality as the ground for law-making and impartiality in ordinary human relationships, precepts governing the latter are obviously not so clear-cut and partiality in particular circumstances is frequently correct (see 290–1).
34. Nietzsche, 1996, 52.
35. Robertson and Merrills, 1996, 2.
36. *Ibid.*, 2–7.
37. Montesquieu is, of course, a title, he inherited a Barony from an uncle, he was born Charles-Louis de Secondat.
38. Rousseau, 1993, 210.
39. *Ibid.*
40. Harvey, 1996, 329–32.
41. Aeschylus, 1999.
42. Kant, 1998, Section 1, 4:393–405, 7–19.
43. The basis of his revolution is summarised in his Introduction to the *Critique of Pure Reason*, Kant, 1934, 25–40.
44. By 'metanarrative' Lyotard means 'subscription to a prevailing theory against whose norms single events of judging might themselves be judged and validated' (Docherty, 1993, 25).
45. Harvey, 1996. Tony Hillerman, *Sacred Clowns*, 1993. Hillerman is a native-American author whose brilliant novels, often detective stories, illustrate the problems faced by native-American people in the USA.
46. For a systematic analysis of urban dispossession see Hardoy and Satterthwaite, 1989.
47. Virgil, *Aeneid*, Book 2.
48. Wisner, 1988, 16.
49. *Ibid.*, 23.
50. It should be noted that figures for the UK are not produced in the sources used by the present authors, but it does not follow that child malnutrition is not a serious problem in that country. In 1996, a major report (*The Hunger Within*, compiled and published by Milk For Schools, the school milk campaign) suggested that 'preliminary indications show approximately 40% of Asian – 30% of Afro-Caribbean – 20% Caucasian children' are faced with nutritional problems (11).
51. See, among many possible examples, Christopher Kirwan in Honderich, 1995, 248–9.
52. Wittgenstein, 1953, Pt. 1, ¶ 255, 91e.
53. The publishers and authors of this accessible encyclopaedia have performed an excellent public service by making it available on the internet (URL: plato.stanford.edu/archives/spr1988/info.html). Its section headed 'Justice, Distributive' is concise, clear and carries a brief, but useful, bibliography.
54. 'Justice as Fairness' in Rawls, 1999.
55. Rawls, 1971, Barry, 1989.

56. Rawls, 1999, 141.
57. Developed by Vilfredo Pareto (1848–1923) this is a gauge of economic efficiency. Pareto suggested that arrangements are optimal only when there is no other possible condition in which at least one person is better off and no one is worse off. Another way of putting it would be to say that a point of Pareto optimality is a situation in which any change which would make one party better off without detriment to the other is impossible. Being 'better off' in any circumstance must incorporate the preferences of the person to be made better off; that is to say that if, within the arrangement, circumstance *A* is to be altered to circumstance *B* to improve the situation of one of the parties, then that party must also prefer *A* to *B*.
58. For those who would like to follow the philosophical steps taken by Braithwaite and Rawls, a clear account of the argument and its importance to any theory of justice may be found in Barry, 1989, 30–95.
59. *Stanford Encyclopaedia of Philosophy*, entry copy by Fred D'Agostino, posted 27 February 1996, modified 28 July 1997.
60. *Ibid.*
61. See Barry, 1989, 374–5.
62. Marx and Engels, 1967, 88, 93.
63. Cockcroft, 1998, 295.
64. Simon, 1997.
65. Cockcroft, 1998, 248.
66. *Ibid.*
67. *Ibid.*, 311–12.
68. See, for example, Marx, 1976, 305, *n.* 19.
69. For examples in Mexico see Cockcroft, 1998. An angry account of the process in India may be found in Arundhati Roy, 1999.
70. Panitch, '"The State in a Changing World": Social Democratising Global Capitalism?' *Monthly Review*, 50 (5), October 1998.
71. Andy Merrifield, 'Class Formation, Capital Accumulation, and the Downsizing of America', *Monthly Review*, 51 (5), October 1999.
72. Eade and Williams, 1995, 9–117.
73. The first figure was an estimate given, in 1990, by Candido Grzybowski in the *Journal of Development Studies*, 26 (4), the second is an estimate offered, in 1991, by Phillip McManus and Gerald Schlabach, in *Relentless Persistence: Non-violent Action in Latin America*; the references are given in Stephen, 1997, 211.

Chapter 6

1. Samuel Beckett, 1959 and 1973.
2. Lenin, 1934.
3. The most notorious case was, of course, the support given by a number of Western NGOs to the genocidal Hutu militias in the Goma refugee

camps. More complex examples may be found in, among other places, Sudan and Kosovo.

4.   UN/US interventions in Somalia are an example of the first and two obvious examples of the latter may be seen in the Narmada dam in India and the Ilisu dam in Turkey.

5.   The Sphere Project has now published *Humanitarian Charter and Minimum Standards in Disaster Response.*

6.   The passages quoted directly and indirectly in this comment on Oxfam's *Handbook* all come from Eade and Williams, 1995, Vol. I, 11–13.

7.   *Ibid.*

8.   Marx, Karl, 1954.

9.   Fowler, 1997.

10. We should probably not be surprised that USAID, a quango rather than an INGO, remained silent on the question, the present authors were unable even to trace a press release from it on the subject.

11. 'The Need for a Radical Alternative: Interview with István Mészáros', *Monthly Review*, 51 (8), January 2000, New York.

12. Eade and Williams, 1995, Vol. I, 20.

13. This clumsy epithet is nearly universal among those involved in humanitarian assistance.

14. Eade and Williams, 1995, Vol. I, 11–15, Vol. II, 799–801.

15. See 'Sins of the Secular Missionaries', *Economist*, 29 January 2000. The author does not see the INGOs' symbiotic relationship with governments as hopelessly compromising, but merely as encouraging NGO self-perpetuation.

16. An example of this phenomenon may be seen in the emergency in Kosovo in 1999. Huge refugee camps with attendant facilities were constructed, there was widespread anxiety among NGOs that medical facilities, provisioning, sanitation, etc. would be inadequate and much fanfare was given to heroic efforts to put matters right. All this took place because that is what humanitarian agencies are expected to do in an emergency. In the event, the camps were substantially redundant as the Kosovan Albanians either found shelter among their extended family networks in Albania or temporarily left the country. *Kosovo Real-Time Evaluation*, ETC-UK, 1999.

17. Examples of all these politicisations of humanitarian assistance may be seen in, among other emergencies, Afghanistan (Danida, 1999, vol. 2), Somalia (IOV, 1994), Sudan (Danida, 1999, vol. 7) and Angola (Danida, 1999, vol. 3).

18. Kim Scipes, 'Global Economic Crisis, Neoliberal Solutions, and the Philippines', *Monthly Review*, 51 (7), December 1999.

19. That dismal distinction belongs to São Tomé and Principe (671.2 per cent).

20. All figures are taken from UNDP, 1999.

21. Posted on USAID's website, December 1999.

22. Deforestation in the Philippines is running at 3.5 per cent per annum (UNDP, 1999).
23. Simon Maxwell, *ODI Poverty Briefing (3): The Meaning and Measurement of Poverty*, London: Overseas Development Institute, February 1999.
24. See Marx and Engels, 1967, 83–4 and Marx, 'Letter to P.V. Annenkov' in Tucker, 1976, 134–42.
25. Plato, 1974, § 358–9, 104 (quoted above in Chapter 5).
26. Stephen, 1997, 56–84.
27. MacEwan, 1999, 193–4.
28. Blaikie, P. (forthcoming), 'A Review of Political Ecology: Issues, Epistemology and Analytical Narratives' in *Zeitschrift für Wirtschaftsgeographie*. Bryant and Bailey, 1997. R.L. Bryant, 'Power, Knowledge and Political Ecology in the Third World: A Review', *Progress in Physical Geography*, 22 (1), 1998, 79–94.
29. Escobar, 1995.
30. For reviews of political ecology, see Peet and Watts, 1996, Peet, 1998.
31. Watts and McCarthy, 1997.
32. Marx and Engels, 1967.
33. Nairn, 2000, 76–80.
34. Guattari, 1984, 219.
35. John Pilger, 'Squeezed to Death', *Guardian*, 4 March 2000.
36. An interesting account of this problem may be found in IOV, 1995. It is all the more compelling because of its source, a government department in a social-democrat state.

References

Aeschylus, 1999, *The Oresteia* (part iii, *The Eumenides*), a new version by Ted Hughes, London: Faber and Faber.

Amin, Samir, 1998, *Spectres of Capitalism: A Critique of Current Intellectual Fashions*, New York: Monthly Review Press.

Arthur, Charles, 1996, 'Confronting Haiti's Environmental Crisis: A Tale of Two Visions' in Collinson, Hellen (ed.), 1996, *Green Guerrillas: Environmental Conflicts and Initiatives in Latin America and the Caribbean*, London: Latin American Bureau.

Barry, Brian, 1989, *Theories of Justice*, Berkeley and Los Angeles: University of California Press.

Beckett, Francis, 1998, (edition consulted), *Enemy Within: The Rise and Fall of the British Communist Party*, Rendlesham: Merlin Press.

Beckett, Samuel, 1959, *Krapp's Last Tape*, London: Faber and Faber.

—— 1973, *Not I*, London: Faber and Faber.

Bernstein, Henry, Crow, Ben, Mackintosh, Maureen and Martin, Charlotte (eds), 1990, *The Food Question: Profits Versus People?* London: Earthscan Publications.

Booth, D. (ed.), 1994, *Rethinking Social Development*, London: Methuen.

Braverman, Harry, 1974 (edition consulted, new edition 1999), *Labor and Monopoly Captial, the Degradation of Work in the Twentieth Century*, New York: Monthly Review Press.

Bryant, R.L. and Bailey, S., 1997, *Third World Political Ecology*, London: Routledge.

Cameron, J.M., 1967, *The Rediscovery of Newman*, London: Sheed and Ward.

Carr, E.H., 1987 (edition consulted), *What Is History?* Harmondsworth: Penguin Books.

Carson, Rachel, 1962, *Silent Spring*, Harmondsworth: Penguin Books.

Chambers, Robert, 1997, *Whose Reality Counts? Putting the First Last*, London: Intermediate Technology Publications.

CNS, a Journal of Socialist Ecology, quarterly, New York: Guilford Publications.

Cockroft, James D., 1998, *Mexico's Hope: An Encounter with Politics and History*, New York: Monthly Review Press.

Cole, Ken, 1995, *Understanding Economics*, London: Pluto Press.

Cole, Ken, Cameron, John and Edwards, Chris, 1983, *Why Economists Disagree: The Political Economy of Economics*, London and New York: Longman.

Commission on Global Governance, The, 1995, *Our Global Neighbourhood*, Oxford: Oxford University Press.

Conroy, Czech and Litvinoff, Miles (eds), 1988, *The Greening of Aid: Sustainable Livelihoods in Practice*, London: Earthscan Publications.

Danida, 1999, *Evaluation of Danish Humanitarian Assistance, 1992–98*, Vols 1–8, Copenhagen: Ministry of Foreign Affairs.

—— Vol. 2, *Afghanistan*.

—— Vol. 3, *Angola*.

—— Vol. 7, *Sudan*.

Deleuze, Gilles, 1983, *Nietzsche and Philosophy*, translated by Hugh Tomlinson, London: The Athlone Press.

Derrida, J., 1978, *Writing and Difference*, translated by A. Bass, London: Routledge and Kegan Paul.

Docherty, Thomas (ed.), 1993, *Postmodernism: A Reader*, New York: Columbia University Press.

Eade, Deborah and Williams, Suzanne, 1995, *The Oxfam Handbook of Development and Relief*, Oxford: Oxfam.

Elson, Diane, 1995, 'Transnational Corporations: Dominance and Dependency in the World Economy' in Corbridge, Stuart (ed.), 1995, *Development Studies: A Reader*, London: Arnold.

Escobar, Arturo, 1995, *Encountering Development: The Making and Unmaking of the Third World*, Princeton, N.J.: Princeton University Press.

Foucault, Michel, 1991 (edition consulted), *Discipline and Punish: The Birth of the Prison*, translated by Alan Sheridan, Harmondsworth: Penguin Books.

Fowler, Alan, 1997, *Striking a Balance: A Guide to Enhancing the Effectiveness of Non-Governmental Organisations in International Development*, London: Earthscan Publications.

Freire, Paulo, 1972, *Pedagogy of the Oppressed*, translated by Myra Bergman Ramos, Harmondsworth: Penguin Books.

Galeano, Eduardo, 1997 (new edition), *Open Veins of Latin America: Five Centuries of the Pillage of a Continent*, translated by Cedric Belfrage, New York: Monthly Review Press.

GATT, 1994, *The Results of the Uruguay Round of Multilateral Trade Negotiations: The Legal Texts*, Geneva: GATT Secretariat.

George, Susan and Sabelli, Fabrizio, 1994, *Faith and Credit: The World Bank's Secular Empire*, Harmondsworth: Penguin Books.

Giddens, Anthony, 1998, *The Third Way: The Renewal of Social Democracy*, Cambridge: Polity Press.

Glacken, C., 1967, *Traces on the Rhodian Shore*, Berkeley: University of California Press.

Goldman, M., 1998, *Privatising Nature: Political Struggles for the Global Commons*, London: Zed Press.

Gray, John, 1998, *False Dawn: The Delusions of Global Capital*, London: Granta.

Guattari, Félix, 1984, *Molecular Revolution: Psychiatry and Politics*, Harmondsworth, Penguin Books.

Hardoy, Jorge E. and Satterthwaite, David, 1989, *Squatter Citizen: Life in the Urban Third World*, London: Earthscan Publications.

Hare, R.M., 1952, *The Language of Morals*, Oxford: Oxford University Press.

Harris, Nigel, 1983, *Of Bread and Guns*, Harmondsworth: Penguin Books.

Harvey, David, 1996, *Justice, Nature and the Geography of Difference*, Oxford: Blackwell.

Hegel, G.W.F., 1952, *Hegel's Philosophy of Right*, translated by T.M. Knox, Oxford: Oxford University Press.

—— 1975, *Aesthetics: Lectures on Fine Art*, translated by T.M. Knox, Oxford: Oxford University Press.

Hill, Christopher, 1988, *A Turbulent, Seditious and Factious People*, Oxford: Oxford University Press.

—— 1992 (edition consulted), *Reformation to Industrial Revolution*, Harmondsworth: Penguin Books.

Hobsbawm, Eric, 1969, *Industry and Empire*, Harmondsworth: Penguin Books.

—— 1995 (edition consulted), *Age of Extremes: The Short Twentieth Century 1914–1991*, London: Abacus Books.

—— 1997, *On History*, London: Weidenfeld and Nicholson.

Holdgate, M.W., Kassas, M. and White, G.F., 1982, *The World Environment, 1972–1982*, Dun Laoghaire: Tycooly International.

Honderich, Ted (ed.), 1995, *The Oxford Companion to Philosophy*, Oxford: Oxford University Press.

Hoskins, W.G., 1955, *The Making of the English Landscape*, London: Hodder and Stoughton.

Hurst, P. and Thompson, G., 1996, *Globalisation in Question*, Cambridge: Polity Press.

Hutton, Will, 1996 (edition consulted), *The State We're In*, London: Vintage.

IOV (Inspectie Ontwikkelingssamenwerking te Velde), 1994, *Humanitarian Aid to Somalia*, Den Haag: Ministerie van Buitenlandse Zaken.

—— 1995, *Evaluation and Monitoring: The Role of Project Evaluation and Monitoring in Netherlands Bilateral Aid*.

IteM (Instituto del Tercer Mundo), bi-annual, *The World Guide*, Oxford: New Internationalist Publications (note: this guide changes its title from time to time, the 1995–96 edition was called *The World*).

IUCN, 1980, *World Conservation Strategy: Living Resource Conservation for Sustainable Development*, Cambridge: IUCN.

James, C.L.R., 1980 (edition consulted), *The Black Jacobins: Toussaint L'Ouverture and the San Domingo Revolution*, London: Allison and Busby.

Kant, Immanuel, 1934 (edition consulted), *Critique of Pure Reason* [1781], translated by J.M.D. Meiklejohn, London: J.M. Dent.

—— 1998 (edition consulted), *Groundwork of the Metaphysics of Morals* [1785], translated by Mary Gregor, Cambridge: Cambridge University Press.

Keynes, John Maynard, 1973 (edition consulted), *The General Theory of Employment, Interest and Money* [1936], London: Macmillan.

Laffan, Brigid (ed.), 1996, *Constitution Building in the European Union*, Dublin: Institute of European Affairs.

Lafferty, William and Eckerberg, Katarine (eds), 1998, *From the Earth Summit to Local Agenda 21: Working Towards Sustainable Development*, London: Earthscan Publications.

LEISA, ILEIA Newsletter, occasional, Leusden: Centre for Research and Information on Low-External-Input and Sustainable Agriculture.

Lenin, V.I., 1934 (edition consulted), *Left-Wing Communism: An Infantile Disorder* [1920], London: Lawrence and Wishart.

Lewis, Martin W., 1992, *Green Delusions: An Environmentalist Critique of Radical Environmentalism*, Durham, N. Carolina and London: Duke University Press.

Lovelock, James, 1995 (edition consulted), *Gaia: A New Look at Life on Earth*, Oxford: Oxford University Press.

Lyotard, J.F., 1984, *The Postmodern Condition: A Report on Knowledge*, translated by G. Bennington and B. Massumi, Manchester: Manchester University Press.

MacEwan, Arthur, 1999, *Neo-Liberalism or Democracy? Economic Strategy, Markets and Alternatives for the 21st Century*, London: Zed Books.

McCabe, Colin, 1985, *Theoretical Essays: Film, Linguistics, Literature*, Manchester: Manchester University Press.

Marx, Karl, 1954, (edition consulted), *The Eighteenth Brumaire of Louis Bonaparte* [1852], London: Lawrence & Wishart.

—— 1973 (edition consulted), *Grundrisse: Foundations of the Critique of Policial Economy (Rough Draft)* [1939–40], translated by Martin Nicolaus, Harmondsworth: Penguin Books.

—— 1975 (edition consulted), *Early Writings*, introduced by Colletti, translated by Rodney Livingstone and Gregor Benton, Harmondsworth: Penguin Books.

—— 1976 (edition consulted), *Capital*, Vol. I [1867], translated by Ben Fowkes, Harmondsworth: Penguin Books.

—— 1978 (edition consulted), *Capital*, Vol. II [1885], translated by David Fernbach, Harmondsworth: Penguin Books.

—— 1981 (edition consulted), *Capital*, Vol. III [1894], translated by David Fernbach, Harmondsworth: Penguin Books.

Marx, Karl and Engels, Frederick, 1965, *The German Ideology*, London: Lawrence and Wishart.

—— 1967 (edition consulted), *Manifesto of the Communist Party* [1848], translated by Samuel Moore (1888), Harmondsworth: Penguin Books.

Mda, Zakes, 1997, *Ways of Dying*, Oxford: Oxford University Press.

Mészáros, István, 1995, *Beyond Capital: Towards a Theory of Transition*, London: Merlin Press.

Middleton, Neil and O'Keefe, Phil, 1998, *Disaster and Development: The Politics of Humanitarian Aid*, London: Pluto Press.

Middleton, Neil, O'Keefe, Phil and Moyo, Sam, 1993, *The Tears of the Crocodile: From Rio to Reality in the Developing World*, London: Pluto Press.

Mill, John Stuart, 1998 (edition consulted), *Three Essays on Religion* [1874], London: Prometheus Books.

Monthly Review, monthly, New York: Monthly Review Foundation.

Naes, A., 1989, *Ecology, Community and Lifestyle*, Cambridge: Cambridge University Press.

Nairn, Tom, 2000, *After Britain: New Labour and the Return of Scotland*, London: Granta Books.

Narotzky, Susana, 1997, *New Directions in Economic Anthropology*, London and Chicago: Pluto Press.

The Netherlands' Ministry of Foreign Affairs Development Cooperation Information Department, 1991, *A World of Difference: A New Framework for Development Cooperation in the 1990s*, The Hague: Ministry of Foreign Affairs.

Newman, John Henry, 1912 (edition consulted), *Apologia Pro Vita Sua* [1864], London: J.M. Dent.

Nietzsche, Friederich, 1996 (edition consulted), *On the Genealogy of Morals* [1887], translated by Douglas Smith, Oxford: Oxford University Press.

—— 1997 (edition consulted), *Daybreak: Thoughts on the Prejudices of Morality* [1881], translated by Maudemarie Clark and Brian Leiter, Cambridge: Cambridge University Press.

Osborn, Derek and Brigg, Tom, 1998, *Earth Summit II: Outcomes and Analysis*, London: Earthscan Publications.

Oxford English Dictionary, 1971, Oxford: Oxford University Press.

Pearce, David (ed.), 1991, *Blueprint 2: Greening the World Economy*, London: Earthscan Publications.

Pearce, David, Markandya, Anil and Barbier, Edward B., 1989, *Blueprint for a Green Economy*, London: Earthscan Publications.

—— 1990, *Sustainable Development: Economics and Environment in the Third World*, London: Earthscan Publications.

Peet, Richard, 1998, *Modern Geographical Thought*, Oxford: Blackwell.

Peet, Richard and Watts, Michael (eds), 1996, *Liberation Ecologies*, London and New York: Routledge.

Pelling, Henry, 1976 (edition consulted), *A History of British Trade Unionism*, Harmondsworth: Penguin Books.

Plato, 1974 (edition consulted), *The Republic*, translated and introduced by Desmond Lee, Harmondsworth: Penguin Books.

Rawls, John, 1971, *A Theory of Justice*, Oxford: Oxford University Press.

—— 1996 (edition consulted), *Political Liberalism*, New York: Columbia University Press.

—— 1999, *Collected Papers*, Cambridge, Mass. and London: Harvard University Press.

Ricardo, David, 1996 (edition consulted), *Principles of Political Economy and Taxation* [1817], Amherst: Prometheus Books.

Robertson, A.H. and Merrills, J.G., 1996 (4th edition), *Human Rights in the World: An Introduction to the Study of the International Protection of Human Rights*, Manchester: Manchester University Press.

Rousseau, Jean-Jacques, 1993 (edition consulted), *The Social Contract and Discourses* [1762], London: J.M. Dent.

Roy, Arundhati, 1999, *The Cost of Living*, London: Flamingo.

Roy, Ash Narain, 1999, *The Third World in the Age of Globalisation: Requiem or New Agenda?* Delhi: Madhyam Books, London: Zed Books.

Simon, Joel, 1997, *Endangered Mexico: An Environment on the Edge*, London: Latin America Bureau.

Smith, Adam, 1974 (edition consulted), *The Wealth of Nations* [1776], Harmondsworth: Penguin Books.

Sogge, David, Biekart, Kees and Saxby, John, 1996, *Compassion and Calculation: The Business of Private Foreign Aid*, London: Pluto Press.

Sphere Project, The, 2000, *Humanitarian Charter and Minimum Standards in Disaster Response*, Oxford: The Sphere Project/Oxfam.

Stephen, Lynn, 1997, *Women and Social Movements in Latin America*, London: Latin America Bureau.

Thompson, E.P., 1980 (edition consulted), *The Making of the English Working Class*, Harmondsworth: Penguin Books.

Thoreau, Henry, 1977 (edition consulted), 'Walden' [1854], in Bode, Carl (ed.), *The Portable Thoreau*, Harmondsworth and New York: Penguin Books.

Tucker, Robert C., 1978 (2nd edition), *The Marx–Engels Reader*, New York: W.W. Norton & Company.

Turner, R.K., Pearce, David and Bateman, Ian, 1994, *Environmental Economics: An Elementary Introduction*, Hemel Hempstead: Harvester Wheatsheaf.

UNDP, annual, *Human Development Report*, New York and Oxford: Oxford University Press.

UNICEF, annual, *The State of the World's Children*, Oxford: Oxford University Press.

UN World Commission on Environment and Development, 1987, *Our Common Future*, Oxford: Oxford University Press.

Vološinov, V.N., 1986 (edition consulted), *Marxism and the Philosophy of Language* [1929], translated by Ladislav Matejka and R. Titunik, Cambridge, Mass. and London: Harvard University Press.

Wahab, Bolanle W., 1996, 'Community Development Associations and Self-reliance: The Case of Isalu Community Development Union, Iseyin, Nigeria' in Blunt, Peter and Warren, Michael D., *Indigenous Organizations and Development*, London: Intermediate Technology Publications.

Ward, Barbara and Dubos, René, 1972, *Only One Earth*, Harmondsworth: Penguin Books.

Watkins, Kevin, 1995, *The Oxfam Poverty Report*, Oxford: Oxfam.

Watts, M. and McCarthy, J., 1997, 'Nature as Artifice, Nature as Artefact: Development, Environment and Modernity in the Late Twentieth Century' in Lee, R. and Wills, J. (eds), *Geography of Economics*, Walton-on-Thames: E.J. Arnold.

WCED (World Commission on Environment and Development), 1987, *Our Common Future*, Oxford: Oxford University Press.

Weber, Max, 1963, *The Sociology of Religion*, London: Methuen.

Whelan, Kevin, 1996, *The Tree of Liberty: Radicalism, Catholicism and the Construction of Irish Identity, 1760–1830*, Cork: Cork University Press.

Wisner, Ben, 1988, *Power and Need in Africa: Basic Human Needs and Development Policies*, London: Earthscan Publications.

Wittgenstein, Ludwig, 1922, *Tractatus Logico-Philosophicus*, translated by C.K. Ogden, London and New York: Routledge & Kegan Paul.

—— 1953, *Philosophical Investigations*, translated by G.E.M. Anscombe, Oxford: Blackwell.

—— 1969 (2nd edition), *The Blue and the Brown Books*, Oxford: Blackwell.

World Bank, annual, *World Development Report*, Oxford: Oxford University Press.

Index

Printed and bound by CPI Group (UK) Ltd, Croydon, CR0 4YY

09/06/2025

14685854-0001

'A roller-coaster ride through competing theories of linguistics, ecological philosophy, economics and redistributive justice'
Green Socialist

Development and assistance in disasters is about helping people to help themselves. It is to do with facilitating 'sustainable livelihoods' and addressing the ills of social discrimination. These seem to be self-evident propositions. In fact, they are a minefield.

If development workers intervene to assist in the creation of environmentally sustainable livelihoods, what judgemental codes are contained in the everyday cultural and linguistic assumptions of development practitioners? If projects are to be sustainable, they must be socially just. By whose justice do we judge?

The authors examine these questions and argue that the assumptions of the social-democratic world, including those of international NGOs, are tied to the perpetuation of capitalism. Neil Middleton and Phil O'Keefe suggest that the issue, in the face of anarchic global financial power, is to rethink the nature of class in a late capitalist world and to recognise indigenous NGOs as the new political vehicles for its struggle.

Neil Middleton was the co-author of *Disaster and Development* (1997) and *Rio Plus Ten* (2003), and the co-editor of *Negotiating Poverty* (2001).

Phil O'Keefe was Professor of Economic Development and Environmental Management at Northumbria University. He was also the Director of ETC-UK and is co-author with Neil Middleton of *Disaster and Development* (1997), *Rio Plus Ten* (2003) and co-editor of *Negotiating Poverty* (2003).

ISBN 9780745316055

9 780745 316055

PLUTO PRESS